BOYINGTON OAK:
A GRAVE INJUSTICE

Mary S. Palmer

An Intellect Publishing Book
www.IntellectPublishing.com

ISBN: 978-1-954693-22-7

First Edition: 2021

V12

Edited by Shannon S. Brown

Cover design and photos: Denis Palmer

Photos: Michael Palmer

The play, also written by Mary S. Palmer, is entitled *The Truth Is in theTree.* It is based on this book and has been produced three times, once at GulfQuest Maritime Museum and twice at Oakleigh Museum House. It is set to be an annual event in Mobile, Alabama

DEDICATION

To all who are charged with dispensing justice. May they temper it with mercy.

TABLE OF CONTENTS

FOREWORD

The legendary true story surrounding the brutal murder of Nathaniel Frost in 1834 near the Church Street Graveyard in Mobile remains an intriguing Southern mystery nearly 200 years later. Nineteen-year-old Charles R. S. Boyington, hanged for the crime of killing his friend and roommate, was buried in the same graveyard where the murder was committed.

I first read about the case while researching and writing an introduction for Mary S. Palmer and Dr. Elizabeth Coffman's book entitled *MemoraMOBILEia: Alabama Gulf Coast Potpourri* (1993).

I had only lived in Mobile a few years, so I had much to learn about the history of the city and its storied past. I spent many hours reading about it in the local history section of Mobile's library and archives. In my research, I came across information about the Boyington Oak and my interest was piqued by the legend of Boyington proclaiming from the scaffold that a live oak would grow from his gravesite to prove his innocence.

The Boyington legend reminded me of a Shakespearean or Greek tragedy with its elements of loyal friendship, betrayal, romance, murder, spiritual and legal battles. It is also a story of unrequited love that Boyington had for Rose, a French baron's daughter. Plus, Baron de Fleur disapproved of their relationship and tried to put a stop to it. But the two lovers ignored his objections and only death separated them. Boyington had great promise of success with his intelligence, musical, and writing talents, but his life was cut short before he was out of his teens.

I kept my notes and research for more than 20 years. I even discussed co-authoring a book about the case with my author friend, Mary S. Palmer. Only one book had been written on the subject, and I believed it deserved another. But, as an inveterate procrastinator, I never wrote it. I knew Mary, who had already published 14 books, was the writer for the job.

Boyington Oak: A Grave Injustice is different from other works of creative non-fiction because of three things. The conviction was based solely on circumstantial evidence. Two jurors did not qualify, but neither was stricken. One was convinced Boyington was guilty before the trial; the other was a British citizen. Also, Boyington claimed an oak tree would grow from his gravesite to prove his innocence. It did.

Years after the crime, interest in the case was revitalized when information revealed led to speculation that an innocent man may have been hanged, an intriguing suggestion of a possible miscarriage of justice for Charles R. S. Boyington. These factors, backed by extensive research, make it unique, timely and timeless, and a fascinating read, appealing to a universal audience.

Maureen Maclay

INTRODUCTION

For My Tomb

Though cold be the earth and stone

Placed over of me what remains;

But there is but one true thought

The earth and stone here has no stains.

The sleep here may be long

And only peace to while the hours;

My life was as a song,

I am not here but among the flowers.

May 1st, 1834, Mobile ROBERT[1]

In November 1833, Charles R.S. Boyington, aka Charles Robert Stuart Boyington, paid his passage from New Haven, Connecticut, to Mobile, Alabama, working as a sailor on the ship Cahaba. Having already served his apprenticeship, he qualified as a journeyman printer, and he traveled South to seek work, claiming to be twenty-three-years-old. Although he had no problem getting a job at Pollard and Dade Printing Company, due to decreased business and other issues, he was soon laid off.

Somehow, Boyington managed to survive. He shared a room with another printer, Nathaniel Frost, in Captain George's Boarding House. Frost suffered from consumption, but whenever he was able, Boyington encouraged his friend to take long walks with him. Their camaraderie on these excursions seemed to raise the sick man's spirits. It also solidified a strong bond of friendship.

Some people noticed how attentive Boyington was to Frost and made comments regarding his *kind and caring* attitude. They interpreted his actions as altruistic. Others questioned Boyington's intentions. Frost was still employed. Was he paying for Boyington's help? Despite speculations, nobody knew the answer.

Charles Boyington met Rose de Fleur at a ball. After a short courtship, they fell in love. Perhaps she knew of the troubles between Charles and his friend Nathaniel Frost; if so, she took that knowledge to her grave. Also, when Frost was murdered, and Boyington was tried for the crime, if Rose had information about what happened, she didn't admit that either. However, even after his death, she remained loyal to her lover, frequently placing flowers on his grave in the shadow of the oak he had vowed would grow on the site to prove his innocence.

The Boyington Oak case has held widespread interest of all who have heard of it throughout its long history. The laxity in following the law had its impact. The way grand jurors were selected in Alabama changed because a non-citizen was on Boyington's jury. The story became a legend that reached far beyond Mobile. Still, a matter frequently discussed, it maintains its essential place as folklore in the annals of time.

Boyington was convicted solely on circumstantial evidence and hanged. Yet, capital punishment remains a controversial ethical issue. Some theologians insist that a pro-life stance is inconsistent with a belief in the death penalty. Both then and now, many people have reservations about capital punishment, which disqualifies them from serving on juries. A more significant debate is that perfect justice requires perfect mercy to prevent innocent people from being condemned to death.

Boyington maintained his innocence with his final words, and the oak tree he vowed would grow from his heart to prove it sprang up on the spot. It still stands, and Boy Scout Troops have featured it in walking tours, and it has been on the Mobile Tree Trail. Is the spirit of Charles R.S. Boyington lurking there? Almost two hundred years later, his secrets lay interred with his bones.

#

February 2019

In the area outside the wall of the Church Street Graveyard, I placed a pink rose at the foot of an ancient oak, beneath its gnarly branches twisted by hurricanes for which Mobile, Alabama is so famous. Time has taken its toll since the acorn first sprouted in 1835 and made roots that broke through the soil on the gravesite of Charles R.S. Boyington. Did its growth fulfill his promise and prove he was innocent of the murder of his friend, Nathaniel Frost?

I gazed at the still strong tree trunk, grown tall, with huge branches and hundreds of roots reaching out in all directions. The sturdy live oak made me wonder. Acorns on the ground reminded me that many oaks volunteered on this site. Hurricanes felled quite a few of them. But was it fate, or coincidence, that this one survived for a hundred and eighty-four years on the exact spot of the convicted murderer's grave in a potter's field?

Glancing at the A.M.E. Methodist Church across the street, I cast my eyes to heaven and asked, "Dear God, can you give me the answer? Was Boyington innocent?" Only a slight breeze sweeping through the trees replied, and I could not decipher what the sound meant.

I pulled Boyington's poem *For My Tomb* out of my pocket and read it for the tenth time. I understood the emotion and appreciated the imagery, but still sought the symbolism's significance and the secrets hidden within, hoping to unearth them and reveal them to the world.

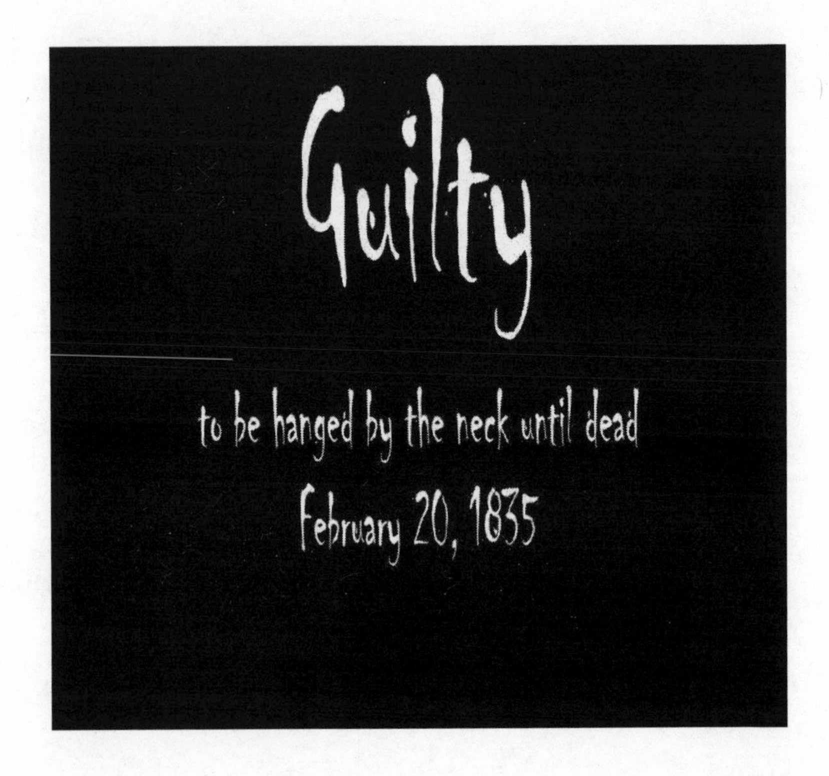

BOYINGTON OAK:
A GRAVE INJUSTICE

ONE

ARRIVING IN MOBILE

November 1833

"You catch on quick. You ought to keep going to sea and move up through the ranks. I could train you to be an engineer," the ship's captain told the young man swabbing the deck. "I figured you for an outdoorsman. Why the hell do you want to get stuck in a job as a printer in a little town like Mobile, Alabama?"

Charles R.S. Boyington didn't respond immediately. He didn't want to admit he was looking for a lawless town. That's why Charles decided to immigrate to Mobile after having a problem with the law as a teenager.[1] But that wasn't the only reason he left his hometown of Litchfield, Connecticut. In a city whose population was less than 3,200, with a decent job, his skill at gambling, and the right connections, he could establish himself and become an entrepreneur, a community leader.

He replied, "I've heard this town is lively. First, I'll have some fun; then, maybe I'll find a wife and settle down."

Captain Arnold put a hand on his hip, "You don't even have a job. Besides, you look like the type to seek adventure."

Charles leaned on his mop. "This *is* my adventure. Ever since printers unionized in 1778 in New York City, even though it didn't last long, we earned respect. Printers are in big demand nowadays. It took a while to learn the trade, and I plan to use my experience."

The captain scratched his bald head. “Okay, it’s your life, Son.” He walked away.

After serving his apprenticeship in New Haven, Connecticut, citing his age as twenty-three-years-old, Charles, certified as a journeyman printer, boarded the ship *Cahaba.* This dark-haired youth with a complexion to match leaned his five-foot-nine-inch frame over the rail and looked out at the water through his small grey eyes.[2] The conversation made him think. A long way from his home and his beloved mother, the adventurer had paid his passage by working as a sailor for Captain Arnold. Cast aside were his brushes with the law, especially the charge of horse stealing in Charleston, South Carolina. Because he was a youth, he’d had minimal consequences for that. Now he was on his way to a bright future in a new area.[3]

He had some help. Reconciled to the fact that Charles wouldn’t stay on as a sailor, the captain took an interest in the affable youth and when the ship docked in Mobile, he obtained work for Charles with the printing company Pollard and Dade.[4]

Charles soon made friends with a co-worker. The two New Englanders, Charles Boyington and Nathaniel Frost, had backgrounds in common. Both were printers, and both were from Connecticut, and they’d soon become roommates.

Before then, Boyington had cultivated the friendship of another printer, George Williamson. He moved to Captain George’s Boarding House on Royal Street to take care of George. It seems Charles Boyington had a penchant for caring for others. It is also evident that he got something in return, as was the case later with Nathaniel Frost, an introvert welcoming companionship at any price.[5]

Charles had no problem integrating into Southern society. When he heard about an upcoming gala ball, he envisioned an opportunity. Savvy beyond his years in the ways of the world, he hustled over to the Red Light District in downtown Mobile, brushing past two scantily-clad women who ogled him as he made his way to a back room where a poker game was taking place.

"I'm Charles Boyington, and I'm new in town. Mind if I join in?" he asked a bearded gentleman twice his age.

"How did you hear about the game?" the man, who smelled of tobacco, demanded.

Charles stuck his thumb over his shoulder. "Little blonde cutie I met at the bar the other night told me."

"Okay. But don't you go around spreading the word about this game, y'hear? It's private. But we can use a fourth tonight. Have a seat," The man puffed cigar smoke. "Be happy to take your money. Name's Tommy John." He did not offer to shake hands; he pointed to his left: "That's Frog and George." Then he dealt the cards, one face down and four up.

"Nice to meet you fellows." When George barely nodded, Charles got the message. He didn't mention that he already knew George Williamson, or that George was the one who told him about the game. It was best not to tip his hand.

Then Frog spoke up. "Hey, ain't you that printer lives at Captain George's Boarding House?"

"Yes, I am."

Frog turned to George. "You lived there, too, didn't you? Wadn't that while you had the flu, or pneumonia, or somethin'? You didn't play with us for a month. And you're a printer, too. Seems like I heard you say somethin' about a friend taking care o' you."

The hand was tipped, and George had to explain. "Right. You have a good memory, Frog. You got me. Charles helped me when

I was sick. *I'm* the one who told him about our game. I wasn't going to say anything till I saw how things went." He chuckled as he pointed to Charles. "He may look young and inexperienced, but don't let that fool you. He's a sharp player. I didn't say anything because I don't want you fellows mad at me if he wins."

"Naw," Tommy John piped up. "Win or lose, we're good sports."

When they had played four rounds, and Charles won the next hand with a pair of fives, Frog didn't prove to be such a good sport. He gathered his cards and threw them down in front of him. "I'm out!" he yelled in his raspy voice. "You ain't takin' no more of my money."

"See ya next week, Frog," Tommy John said.

"Maybe not." Frog slung on his coat and headed for the door.

"Yeah, you'll be right here." Tommy John guffawed as the door slammed behind Frog.

Half an hour later, his laughter subsided. At the end of the last hand, no one at the table was smiling. Except Charles. He collected his winnings with a broad grin. "By the way," he said to his seatmate, "I hear there's a big event, a ball at a local hotel or something, coming up soon. Since I'm new in town, I'd like to meet some, uh, refined young ladies. Could you arrange for me to be invited?"

"Har, har, har!" Tommy John gave Charles a hefty slap on the back. "Son, you got a lotta nerve. First you take my money, then you ask for a favor." He threw up his hands. "But what the hell. I'll see to it."

The next week a neatly addressed envelope bearing a formal invitation to the dance at the Alabama Hotel on the corner of Saint Francis and Royal Streets was delivered to the young printer at

Captain George's Boarding House. With a bit of finagling, Charles had taken his first step toward acceptance into Mobile society.

To attend, he had to have proper attire. Using his poker winnings along with some financial assistance from Nathaniel, he managed to purchase the necessary formal wear. A social climber, he knew this was the way to meet the "best" people. Since Mobile society was fluid, obtaining an invitation to these dances sponsored by prominent families was not difficult.[6]

As Charles prepared to leave the boarding house for the Alabama Hotel that evening, he patted some witch hazel on his cheeks, took one last glance in a hand-held mirror, and adjusted his collar.

"I hope to meet the belle of the ball tonight, Nathaniel," he told his friend as he turned away from the stench of pillows soaked with phlegm.

Propped up in bed, Nathaniel glanced up from the book he was reading. "With that stylish black jacket and your charm, I have no doubt you'll soon get a wife."

Boyington's smile exposed a set of straight, white teeth. He tipped his top hat to his roommate. All he was missing to be completely in style was a walking cane, but he trusted he'd have a fine one in short order—with a few more winning hands of poker at the backroom casino.

Frost closed his book. "You're attending the fancy ball, and I'm stuck in this boarding house coughing my head off. No matter, it's the way of the world. Just dandy." Frost turned on his side, faced the faded yellow wallpaper and muttered, "Have a good time."

Outside, the December air was chilly, so Charles buttoned his coat. He passed green lawns and bright pink azaleas blooming early because of the mild winter. He marveled at the old live oak trees with massive trunks and broad branches spanning out in all directions, fully draped with delicate, wispy streamers of olive-colored Spanish moss.

Reminiscing about his family in Connecticut, he pictured them huddled around the fireplace wearing winter clothing at their Litchfield home after a hearty meal cooked by his mother. Soon, snow would blanket the fields and hillsides of his childhood while he worked to establish himself in this semi-tropical climate, worlds away and surrounded by unfamiliar wonderment. He'd survive and thrive. Mobile's lawlessness allowed him to gamble and earn money, enabling him to buy the proper clothing to participate in its culture.

The intense feeling of nostalgia that ran through him dissipated as it collided with the rush and excitement of attending the ball in this bustling city, a city of new beginnings for him.

Along the way, couples out for an evening stroll nodded and said, "Hello," and Boyington felt glad to be alive. He straightened his naturally erect posture and strutted along.

The hotel exuded laughter and music as Boyington made his way to the ballroom through the crowded lobby of well-dressed couples greeting each other with hugs and handshakes.

The mood of high spirits was contagious, but he saw not one familiar face. He knew he was an outsider but smiled with the unflappable spirited ease and energy of youth, confident and undaunted.

Once inside the ballroom, he surveyed the scene and sucked in his breath. He'd never seen such an elegant and opulent space. In the Puritan culture of Connecticut, Christmas wasn't celebrated. It was frowned upon. Here, the theme of the season showed everywhere. In December 1833, the ballroom was filled with Christmas decorations. Stockings hung from mantels covered with pinecones and greenery. A ceiling-height tree in one corner was full of fruit and lit candles. A tree made of magnolia branches decorated another corner. Mistletoe hung from chandeliers. Pinecones were interspaced between greenery on tables amidst sterling silver plates of hors d'oeuvres of every variety. These were being devoured, followed by Champagne offered by male and female Negro servers, clad in black and white, who seemed to be everywhere with trays full of crystal glasses.

Boyington was thankful his mother insisted on his taking dancing lessons while he was in high school. He'd need to remember the steps to the Virginia Reel and the waltz to impress the southern belles.

At this ball, Boyington planned to insert himself into Mobile society. The music faded to a stop, and the dance floor cleared. He looked around and spotted a young lady who immediately caught his attention. She stood in a corner beside an older woman who was adjusting the ruffled collar of the younger girl's off the shoulder gown, pulling it up a bit. The center of his attention exuded grace as she chatted with friends, and her beauty enthralled him; it was enhanced by the winter rose atop her crown of chestnut brown curls. Her bespangled ivory silk dress with an empire waist and trimmed in blue imported lace accentuated her slim figure.[7]

When Charles approached, he almost stepped on the hem of the young lady's skirt. He made a deep bow, drawing the tail of his richly decorated evening coat above his knees. "I am sorry. May I introduce myself? I am Charles R.S. Boyington." He knew the rules of etiquette required a formal introduction, but he bypassed them. "If your dance card isn't full, may I have the pleasure of this dance?"

"Why…"

The lady with her interrupted. "I am Mademoiselle Marie Lydia Justin, Miss Rose de Fleur's chaperone."[8] She cast her eyes upon his attire, first focusing on his lacy shirt, then sizing him up and down. She tapped her finger on her lips. "Are you new to our city, Sir?"

Charles nodded. "I am, Ma'am. Charles Boyington, at your service." Without further ado, he took Miss de Fleur's hand and escorted her to the floor where he showed his expertise at the waltz the orchestra played. His led and his partner followed, keeping in perfect step.

Between the first and second dance, Charles took his partner to the punch table and then over to a quiet corner. "Christmas is wonderful here in Mobile," he told her. "You celebrate much more than we do up North." He took her hand. "Would you do me the honor of allowing me to recite a Christmas poem to you? I came across it recently. It was published anonymously because the professor who wrote it considered it unscholarly, and he didn't want his name—Clement Clark Moore—associated with it." He cracked a crooked smile. "But his friend took it to the *Troy Sentinel,* and they published it December 23, 1823."[9]

He took a deep breath. "It's called, *A Visit from Saint Nicholas:*

'Twas the night before Christmas, when all through the house, not a creature was stirring, not even a mouse. The stockings were hung by the chimney with care, in hopes that St. Nicholas soon would be there." The band played, and the music drowned out his voice.

Rose clapped. "What a lovely poem, Mr. Boyington. I am a child at heart." She put her empty cup on a table. "Oh, the music's started again." They returned to the dance floor, where he reveled in the delicate scent of a winter-blooming gardenia in Rose's hair.

After the Virginia Reel, during a waltz, Charles found out a few things about his new acquaintance. He learned her father was a Napoleonic refugee and that she was nineteen years old. Her beautiful azure eyes and warm smile mesmerized him. He knew he had met the love of his life.

To impress her with his musical talent, he asked the orchestra leader to allow him on stage, and he joined them in playing the lute. His performance produced the desired result; Rose clapped for a full minute. Then they joined the crowd gathered around the piano and sang three verses of *The Snow Bird's Song*:

Oh, the Snow Bird! Oh, the Snow Bird!

It's crowned with flakes of snow;

It flits here, it flits there,

And every where you go!

It sings of love! It sings of love!

Then press your heart to mine;

My darling! My darling!

My love in you I find!

Oh, the Snow Bird! Oh, the Snow Bird!

His heart is true and kind;

He whispered in my ear and said,

"We must our hearts combine!"

Charles squeezed Rose's hand. "Ah, my dear Miss de Fleur; you have a beautiful voice. I've never heard anything so lovely." He looked into her eyes while she fluttered her eyelashes at him.

To follow protocol and avoid being too aggressive, after four dances, he returned Miss de Fleur to her chaperone. With thanks and "I hope to see you again soon," he excused himself and departed with a bow.

As he crossed the ballroom floor, Charles glanced around, looking for the man who'd provided him with the invitation to thank him, but he didn't see Tommy John anywhere. Elated at his encounter with the lovely young lady, he didn't carry out his intention to meld into Mobile society that night. Instead, he headed for home to bask in his happy mood.

Ignoring his snoring roommate, Charles slipped into his nightgown. Before retiring, he sat on the edge of his bed and took out the best handmade writing paper available.[10] By the light of a flickering candle which also helped diffuse the room's unpleasant scents, he wrote the first verse of a poem;

TO A BUTTERFLY AT CHRISTMAS

Oh, care-free creature,

Flitting here and flitting there;

You should be tucked in

From this chilly air.[11]

But he fell asleep and didn't finish it. The next day he sent Rose a letter in his clear handwriting, without flourishes:

Dear Mademoiselle Rose,

We met last night for the first time, and I cannot express to you what pleasure this meeting gave me. I cannot recall an evening spent so joyously. Everyone at the ball seemed so courteous and friendly to me. Even as I slept like an angel, you came to me in my dream. I can hear now the rustle of your silk dress, as like an agile gazelle your graceful step pranced o'er the ballroom floor until I felt like I was on the greenward [sic] surrounding Titania's flowery throne; and I like Oberon, bowed to your every wish and crowned your brow with rosebuds. Yes, yes, you were beautiful, and I can say as Shakespeare did in The Taming of the Shrew,

"She's not forward, but modest as the dove:

She's not hot, but temperate as the morn'.

She's beautiful, and therefore to be wooed;

She is a woman, therefore to be won."

Your sweet song of the snow birds, in your clear, sweet soprano voice, reminded me of the long snows back home in Connecticut and the gay [carefree] young folks as they slid o'er the ice in eve'n time, and the sleigh bells tingling their merry sounds along the country roads, echoing and re-echoing through the woods. The song brought into my heart memories I left behind. But I have met you, and happiness is now again with me.

I long for the next opportunity to play for you to sing, each strain and note of your song brought thrills into my very soul, and my heart swelled and throbbed as I held your arm and hand in mine as we danced and bowed in the graceful minutes.

I am awaiting with impatience the time when I will be permitted to see you again and sit and talk with you in the moonlight, or stroll with you through the pleasant and flowery fields and woods around Mobile. We'll sit and listen to the birds as they flit from bough to bough with sweet song.

O, that this pleasure will be soon again, my lovely Rose! And until that moment the waiting will seem a hundred years or more. Until then, sweet Rose, I remain

Your ardent admirer,

BOYINGTON[12]

Her reply came swiftly. Her handwriting appeared cramped, and it had some flourishes:

Dear Mr. Boyington,

Your letter was handed to me today by my cousin, Mademoiselle Marie Justin (Lydia), who received it from the postcarrier. Kindly do not post any more letters, send them if you can. I will explain my reasons for this request. You are flattering me; however, I am glad the 'Snow Bird's Song' pleased you; but I am equally charmed with your playing the harpsichord and the lute. Madame Caro [a member of the colonial family of Mobile, Pensacola and New Orleans] played her operatic selections with ease and charm. I am told by Mademoiselle Justin, who has conversed with Captain William George, that you equally perform on the mandolin and harp as you do on the lute. You cannot call to see me until I tell you, as I must confess to you my father is opposed to my receiving company, and has appointed my cousin Mademoiselle Justin as duenna, so when we meet again alone I will appoint the place and let you know by the slave boy. However, my cousin has consented to chaperone several friends for a party to go into the woods on Monday evening to gather nuts and wild flowers, and she has permitted me to ask you to join us, since she will be with us.

Do not think ill of what I write in regards to our meeting each other. I will further explain.

"Hope is a lover's staff, we walk hence with that,

And manage it against despairing thought."

Until we meet again.

Mobile, Dec. 7th, 1833

ROSE[13]

After reading the encouraging quote from Shakespeare's *The Two Gentlemen of Verona,* Boyington promptly replied, "May I address you 'Rosa, my dear,' in my future notes?" He also said he would meet her after Mass and they'd go to her friend Barbara's home where he was invited to dinner. The route would evade Rose's father, if her father happened to attend the Mass, too. It was a big concession for him to attend those services. He admitted that he didn't attend religious services and had never been in a Catholic church. But he would do almost anything to be near Rose.

His thoughts turned to a romantic scene: Mobile would soon have gas streetlights, and the theater would be lit with sperm oil lamps. How nice it would be. But he didn't elaborate on those things to Rose. Instead, he bragged a bit, telling her about buying a new suit from St. John, Price & Co.—a Jackson coat of green and Oxford mixed cloth—pantaloons striped, corded mixed color with light cord, vest Florentine of ivory color dotted with tiny fleur-de-lis designs and blue buttons. He also described his new overcoat, and black imported boots, saying his mother sent him the money to purchase those clothes. He stated that when he wore them, she'd be the first to observe them.

He promised her something, too, an exquisite yellow and black mantilla his friend brought him from the West Indies. "It will be sent with this letter by Messrs. Pollard & Dade's negro delivery boy," he said. "He will put them in the third pew at 2 o'clock."

It ended with a declaration of love: "My heart swells up in throbs of love for thee, sweet Rose, and like a lovely flower I shall see you in my dreams tonight."

Rose acknowledged his letter by giving him permission to call her Rosa, my dear. Then she told him she'd also received the mantilla and only her slave woman Delphine had seen it. Delphine had begged her to put it 'around my shoulders, jes fo' a minute'. Rose said she complied, and then she draped it around her own shoulders, pretending "to be Empress Josephine receiving Napoleon on his return from the battlefield.[15] The December 10, 1833 letter was cut short because Mademoiselle Justin was coming.

#

Despite their intense attraction to each other, things in Charles's love life did not go smoothly. Although they had not met, Baron de Fleur did not approve of his daughter keeping company with a printer. He let his feelings be known right away. He made every effort to keep them apart, but Rose's chaperone, who was also her cousin, sympathized with the young lovers. When Charles discovered Rose attended Mass each morning at the Catholic Cathedral on Conti Street, he, too, became a regular.

Lydia, a romantic, passed notes between the two during the service. The first Bishop of Mobile, Michael Portier, who said the Mass, either didn't notice or ignored their actions. With Lydia's help, the two managed to exchange letters delivered by slaves, and they met secretly for walks, often catching butterflies, the custom of the times.[16]

Charles spent much of his income as a printer dressing for the part of a successful man in attire such as satin pantaloons and double-breasted velvet vests. To supplement that income, he lived by his wits, including exploiting his friend. At the mercy of consumption, Frost appreciated Charles's assistance and lent him money. Also, by gambling and winning more than he lost, Charles managed to buy stylish clothes, even after he'd been unemployed for several weeks.[17]

On one of their strolls, permitted by chance when Rose's father was away from home, Charles used the opportunity to entertain her by telling of his experience working as a sailor to earn his passage from New Haven to Mobile. "During a storm, we faced some rough seas. I almost got thrown overboard once," he bragged.

"That is so exciting." Her eyes widened. "You are an adventurer. Not like me. After we left France and settled in Mobile, I have never been anywhere. What wonderful experiences you have had."

Rose stopped walking, covered her mouth with her hand, and the conversation took a turn. "My father calls you *un homme du monde.*"

"Does he know I'm a printer by trade?"

"Yes. If you like that work, Charles, I don't see a problem." She lowered her eyes. "But Papa does," she whispered.

Charles raised his brows. "Ah, so it seems I have been investigated. It does not surprise me that the Baron has made queries. It is natural that he wants to protect his lovely daughter." He cocked his head. "I suppose he's right. I am a man of the world. So your father does not approve of my occupation. *Il ne fait rien.*"

Rose fluttered her eyelashes. She turned to her companion. "You understand a little French, no? We always speak it at home. As for my father, he never approves of any of my suitors." Placing her arm in the crook of his, she leaned closer and whispered in his ear, "You used the expression correctly, it does not matter. This time, I do not care, either. I will continue to meet you, Charles, no matter what my father says." She looked back at her chaperone a few feet behind them. "With my cousin's help, we can manage." She twirled one of her curls. "In fact, I'm going to invite you to Christmas dinner at my house. When my father meets you, I'm sure he'll understand why I, uh, like you so much. Will you come? Please say yes."

"Yes." Charles squeezed her hand and led her toward a wooden slatted bench in Bienville Square. They sat, but Lydia did not join them. She chose a bench in sight of them on the other side of the park.

"An old Spanish hospital used to be on this site." Rose pointed to the corner of Conception and Dauphin Streets. "Now it's deeded to always be a park. And the city is buying more space in the area as it becomes available."

Raising her hand to his lips, he kissed it. "Ah, Rosa, my dear, your intelligence is equaled only by your loveliness. Most young women take no interest in civic affairs; where did you learn all those things?"

Her blue eyes met his. "I had a tutor and, despite his overprotection of me, my father is progressive. Unlike many men today, he believes women should be educated."

"And I agree." Taking a slip of paper out of his knee-length britches, Charles read aloud:

TO ROSE

I saw a lovely butterfly

Light on the bosom of a winter rose;

He kissed the stamens one by one,

Then flew away as in a love-sick pose.

Each eve I came into the garden

To look upon this lovely flower;

And came to me the sudden thought,

"I'll place it in my lady's bower."

The raindrops beat down the rose

Until it hung its lovely head,

And when I returned the next eve

I found, too, the butterfly was dead.

So if I had been the butterfly
And you the lovely winter rose,
I would do the same, methinks,
And call down the blinding snows!

True love is the greatest thing
In life a man can own,
Oh, 'tis you, my lovely Rose,
I love and you alone!

Glancing to be sure the chaperone was not looking, with a kiss on Rose's cheek, Charles vowed in a whisper, "It is true, it is you I love and all I want, Rosa, my dear."

Rose blushed, but she did not pull away. "Thank you, Charles, the poem is beautiful. I adore it. Its music echoes in my ears. I'll dream of your words tonight."

"Rosa, my dear," Charles repeated his pet name for her, "I'll dream of *you* tonight."[18]

TWO

SECRET MEETING

One morning as Rose dressed for Mass which she attended almost daily, her maid tightened the strings of her corset. “You sho’ is tiny, Miss Rose. Meybe I needs to fix you a bigga breakfast when you gits back from church.”

“Oh, Ellie,” Rose replied, “I never eat that much.” As the buxom teenager twice her size slipped the puffy-sleeved day dress over Rose’s head and she wiggled into it, she recalled when her father had bought the fatherless Tunger family—a mother and two children. Essie Mae had pleaded that they not be separated. Ellie was her age, and the son, Dyer, a frail boy, was two years younger. A week after the purchase for $95, the sickly Dyer died. Unlike the Christian Mass held for her own brother, Robert, Dyer had no funeral service. The only ceremony was a solo Negro spiritual sung by his mother. He was buried without a coffin in a shallow grave behind the slave quarters on their property.

Lydia strolled into the room, interrupting her morbid thoughts. “Almost ready, Rose? We better leave.”

As Ellie hooked the last button on the back of her dress, Rose picked up her fan festooned with multicolored butterflies and folded it closed. “It is only a ten-minute walk, Lydia, no hurry.” The grandfather clock in the hall chimed six times. “But if we arrive early, maybe my friend will be there.”

Ellie took a step back and giggled.

“What is funny, Ellie?”

Ellie blinked. “Oh, nuthin’, Miss Rose, nothin’ t’all.”

As Lydia walked by her side to the Cathedral on the south side of Conti Street, she handed Rose a note which said, “Rosa, my dear, I will be at Mass this morning. I hope we can take a walk. There is a place I visit often that I want to show you. It is a beautiful spot.”

Rose wondered if it had anything to do with a letter he’d written saying “Here am I writing to you as though you were miles away, and not right here in Mobile…The big oak tree will be telling our secrets, which the world must know sooner or later.” Rose shivered. Big oak—sooner or later—those words seemed like a foreshadowing of some sort.

Lydia interrupted her thoughts. “I told your father you and I would take a long walk after Mass and that we would be late for breakfast.” She grinned. “I did not tell him anyone else would be going along with us.”

Rose hugged Lydia. “You are so sweet. My father does not understand. He thinks Charles could not take care of me. But I do not care. I—I—, well, I care for Charles.” Her eyes pleaded for compassion as she looked at her companion. “But you understand, I think.”

Lydia nodded. “I am a lot older than you, but I was young once.” She stared into the distance. “And in love. My family did not approve, and they forced my suitor away.”

Narrowing her eyes, Rose gripped Lydia’s arm. “And you never married. That is sad, Lydia.”

They reached the church and ascended the steps. Rose did not have to look far to spot Charles in the back pew. Genuflecting, she slid in next to him, but Lydia squeezed between them, whispering to Rose, "We do not want anyone to talk." As soon as they were seated, Charles handed Lydia a note and pointed to Rose.

Holding the paper low in her lap, Rose read: "Rosa, my dear, I spent the night thinking of being with you today. I look forward with joy to the pleasure of your company after the services." Rose leaned forward and winked at Charles as she slipped the note into her pocket. Then the bells rang as two altar boys led Bishop Michael Portier down the aisle.[1] The Latin Mass only lasted twenty minutes. As they left the church, Lydia made sure Charles kept his distance behind them until they turned the corner out of sight of curiosity seekers ready to spread gossip about the Baron's family.

Charles caught up with Rose and Lydia in the second block. "Where are we going? Where is this 'beautiful spot' you want to show me? Come on, tell me," Rose teased.

Charles took her arm and placed it in his. "Do not be impatient, Rosa, my dear. It is not far—perhaps a mile." He looked at her pale blue dress, perfectly fitting her wasp waistline. "Ah, blue becomes you. How lovely you look this morning, more beautiful than the place I am taking you to see." He faced her and walked backward, still holding onto her arm. "Or perhaps *it* is beautiful as a work of nature, and *you* are beautiful as a creature." He stepped back to her side. "If I believed in God, I would have said 'as a creature of God.'"

Rose's eyes widened. "We just left church. Are you telling me you are an atheist?"

Holding up a palm, he explained. "I came to church to be with you. Perhaps, I consider myself more of an agnostic."[2]

Rose stopped. "Are you simply trying to appease me, Charles?"

"Oh, no, you are much too bright to be fooled by me, Rosa, my dear."

She grimaced. “My religion is important to me.”

Grasping both of her hands in his, he added, “And anything, *anything*, important to you is important to me.” He pointed to a home under construction in the distance. “We have arrived. Look over yonder at that magnificent construction.”

“It will be a lovely home when it is completed. Look at the galleried porch. I bet it will be a Greek Revival style.”

Charles spun her around toward a stand of trees. “But here’s what I really wanted you to see.”

“Ah, how lovely!” Rose gasped, placing her hand above her heart when she saw the magnificent live oaks surrounding them. The hundreds of years old branches hung low and many cascaded over a wide area.

“It’s amazing how a one-inch acorn escapes hungry squirrels and grows.” She picked one up and fingered it. “These fall by January first. You can step on one, and if you push that little barrel-shaped seed with its reddish brown, hairy scales one inch into this fertile soil, it will germinate. Its taproot grows down, and it sends a shoot upward in a few weeks, but it takes seventy-five years to reach its mature size.” She pointed all around. “These trees may have been here when Mobile was founded in 1702.”

Cocking his head, Charles looked at her. “And how does a pretty girl like you know so much about trees, Rosa, my dear?”

She fluttered her eyelids. “I read a lot, Charles.”

“I see. I’m impressed. Well, do you also know the scientific name of the live oak is quercus virginiana?”

She grinned. “I do. But how do *you* know that? You’re new to our area.”

"I read a lot, too." He chuckled. "But to be honest. I learned it from a story we printed about oaks at Spring Hill College when it was founded in 1830, and those on the property of that new Catholic monastery out on Springhill Avenue."

"Oh, you mean the Convent of the Visitation. I visit there frequently. When Bishop Portier became aware of the lack of schools in his diocese, he received permission from Pope Gregory XVI to found the convent. He rented a five-room house, remembering the work of the Visitation nuns in his native France, he recruited five nuns from Georgetown, Washington, D.C., and they sailed here, arriving in Mobile in December 1832."

"I'm not Catholic, nor do I profess any religion, as you know." He shrugged. "But I am interested in history. We printed a story on that convent, too. It impressed me that forty pupils enrolled in the first year."

Rose nodded. "By January 1833, they were well-established, and a building was erected. Nice architecture. Lovely oaks there, too. " She took Charles' hand. "Even if we differ about religion, we have a lot in common. We're both interested in history and nature. Let's see what else is here."

A footpath worn by former visitors made it possible to walk through the woods without having to shove scrub brush aside.

"It appears many people have found this place before, and they have worn a path for us." He walked ahead, stopping behind the trunk of a huge tree out of Lydia's sight. "Look at all the magnolia trees, and those azalea plants remind me that some of your people from France contributed to the beauty. Oh, I heard the house will be called *Oakleigh*. James W. Roper, a slave trader and a cotton broker, is having it built."[3]

"Yes, Papa said Roper has eighteen slaves; he's a rich man. He imports his own flowers. Papa knew one of the men who brought those azaleas here in the middle of the last century. He also told me about the Louisiana Purchase when all the territory between the Mississippi River and the Rocky Mountains was sold to the United States by France for three cents per acre. But he has not mentioned this magnificent house. How do you know all about that?"[4]

"I have friends who keep me apprised of many things, Rosa, my dear."

Rose nodded. "I see, Charles. Oh, by the way, since you have a pet name for me, I should like to have one for you. What does the 'R' in your name stand for?"

"Robert."

"I like that. It suits a person gifted with the ability to write poetry." And it reminded her of her brother, also named Robert, who died in France.

"So, we think alike. I often sign my poetry with the name Robert." He winked at her. "But since it's a pen name, let's keep it a secret."

She looked around to see Lydia facing another direction and then edged closer to Charles, her chin raised as she gazed into his eyes. "All right, I'll still call you Charles most of the time, but in my prayers and thoughts, you shall be Robert."

He pulled her to him and kissed her on the lips. Her body fell limp in his arms.

"Rose, Mr. Boyington," Lydia called out. "Where are you?"

Rose backed away from Robert and stepped forward where Lydia could see her. "We're right here, Lydia, admiring the beauty of this forest."

“Well, come on, you two, we had better be getting back. Your mother will be worried.” She motioned them to follow her. “Breakfast will be ready, and you do not want to miss it.”

Rose let Charles place her arm in his again, and she looked up at him with dreamy eyes, whispering, “I do not care if I miss breakfast, Charles; I would rather spend more time with you.”

Charles sighed as he looked back at her. “Ah, Rosa, my dear, the feeling is mutual. It certainly is.”

Lydia stepped a few yards ahead of them, walking at a faster pace. They parted ways when they reached Government Street, but not without a promise to meet the next morning.

“I care for you very much,” Rose said. “I will await tomorrow with great anticipation.”

Charles squeezed her hand. “Until tomorrow, Rosa, my dear.”

“Moi, aussi, dear Charles.” Taking out a lace handkerchief, Rose dubbed away the tears forming on her cheeks.

“Rose, please come, we must go.” Lydia’s voice was insistent.

Taking a few steps backward while blowing kisses to her love, Rose complied with her chaperone’s order.

THREE

NEW FRIEND

Back at Captain George's Boarding House, Charles encountered no one in the hall or the kitchen. Nathaniel had left for work, so he was also alone in his room. Charles had given his friend a message for Mr. Pollard saying he had pressing business and wouldn't be in until noon. Taking out a packet of papers secured by a thin ribbon, he untied the bow and spread them on the desk. On top was a flyer asking for help finding a horse thief—one Charles Boyington. He stared at the offer of a reward of $25.[1] "I am worth more than that," he said aloud. He cringed at recalling reports also stating they'd caught up with him and hethat he "was arrested for horse stealing in Savannah early in 1833."[2]

Flopping the paper face down, and disturbing thoughts swirled through his mind. *Rose is bright. She knows about history. What if she finds out I'm an accused horse thief and I could be disenfranchised? I cannot let her find out. She would never see me again, no matter how I protest or try to explain the circumstances.* He scanned the room. *I am not sure my locked box is safe. What is a better place to hide it?* He laid his head on the flyer, and his thoughts turned to the day he rode off on that horse.

The incident actually happened on the outskirts of New Haven. Charles, age sixteen, had gone fishing with a couple of friends from the South who'd come North hoping to find their fortunes. On the way back, they passed a vacant house and stopped behind a barn to smoke hand-rolled cigars. When they heard a horse neigh, one boy jumped up. “You hear that? I thought this place was deserted.”

“Well,” Charles said, “we didn’t catch anything. Maybe we ought to take that horse home with us.” He walked to the barn and saw a skinny mare. “You hungry, fellow?” He turned to his friend. “I don’t see any food. Wonder if anybody’s taking care of him?”

“There’s a saddle hanging on the wall.”

The second boy grinned. “Yeah, Charles. You game enough to take a ride? Ha, ha, bet you don’t have the nerve.” the third boy said.

Charles went into the stall, removed the saddle and slung it on the horse. “How much do you want to bet?” He led the horse out into the barn and hopped on it. Without warning, the horse dashed out of the barn with the two boys following.

As the horse galloped along, a shot rang out. It missed Charles by inches. He turned to see a man standing on the porch of the house they thought was vacant yelling obscenities followed by, “You won’t get far, anyhow. I’ll sic the law on you.”

Charles saw his friends scrambling into the woods, and he kept riding. By the time he got far enough away from the house to hide, sweat poured off his body, and he was shaking all over. Worse yet, he had paid no attention to the direction the horse headed. He yelled, “Whoa!” When the horse stopped, he dismounted and looked around. He realized he had no idea where he had ended up.

With his natural ability and survival skills, Charles hid in the woods a couple of days. Once, he heard a large number of riders, Under cover of the thick undergrowth, he watched six men on horseback gallop by, probably a posse on his trail. He got water for himself and the horse from the creek they’d fished in. And he lived on what he knew to be edible berries. In a farmer's field, he found some hay to feed the horse.

While in an exhausted sleep one night, a man pulled him to his feet and stuck a shotgun in his face. "Gottcha!" the man called out. They tied his wrists with rope, put him on a horse with a member of the posse and took him to jail in New Haven.

After one day of pacing the floor in a six-foot square cell he shared with a drunk, both of which stunk of urine, he knew confinement was not for him. But he could find no immediate way out. In jail, while awaiting his trial, he spent time adding to his poker-playing skills. Before his day in court came up, the horse's owner said because of the thief being underage, he would not ask for the death penalty. The guilty verdict stipulated that Charles would work off his fine in the cotton fields for a year's hard labor.[3]

It did not take long for Charles to get out of that predicament. His charisma paid off. He made friends with the foreman and, with his expertise, the cardsharp soon had the foreman in debt to him. To settle it, they made a deal. The foreman's brother owned a print shop, and Charles was sent there to serve an apprenticeship as a printer. He caught on fast, but it still took several years.

During that time, the courts debated whether he was free legally or not. To avoid being hauled back into court for the offense and retried, as soon as Charles became a journeyman printer, he left New Haven and headed to the Deep South, out of the clutches of the law.[4]

Charles lifted his head and rubbed the nape of his neck. Those long-ago memories reminded him of his vulnerability. He could not let Rose know anything about his clash with the law. He would have to direct conversations to avoid controversial subjects. Since Rose was smart, this might not always be easy. But he would find a way.

After another glance around the room, for lack of a better option, Charles put his papers, including the *Wanted* flyer back in his box. He locked it and stuck the key in his pocket. Then he put the box in the drawer, placing his underwear on top of it.

#

Charles did not have to worry about any undesirable conversation topic the next morning. Rose's mother sat next to her in the church pew. When Charles entered, he sat on the opposite side of the aisle. Lydia nodded at him, and Rose winked as she held her fan close to her face. After Communion, which Charles abstained from, he left. Outside, he motioned to a young black boy.

"Yassuh?" the boy said as he approached.

Charles pulled out a piece of paper and scribbled on it. "You wait here until the people leave church. Sneak this to the tallest of the three ladies who will come out together." He handed the boy a couple of pennies and shook his finger at him. "I'll be watching. Be sure you give it to the right one, or I'll have your hide."

The boy's head bobbed up and down. "No, suh, I means yassuh. I won't make no mistake. Thank ya."

Charles crossed the street and stood behind a tree. When the boy slipped the note to Lydia, Charles left the scene whistling, confident his wishes would be fulfilled and anticipating meeting his love that afternoon.

Six hours later, after working half a day, he took long strides down Government Street to his destination—the Church Street Cemetery, surrounded by a high wall people believed would keep germs from infecting citizens.[5] On the way, in an area where horse dung carpeted the streets with a warm brown matting, he stepped into a pile of it. Swearing, he scraped it off in the grass. He didn't want to meet Rose smelling of manure.

When he arrived at the graveyard and looked around, Rose and Lydia were nowhere in sight. He wrung his hands. Had his note been lost, ignored? Did Rose's father intercept the message and forbid her to come? He looked up and down Government Street; no one was in sight. Charles sat in the shade of a magnolia tree and lit a cigar, his last one. Playing poker tonight would provide money to buy others. On the third puff, someone tapped him on the shoulder.

"Good evening, Charles." Rose's melodious voice made him sigh in relief.

He stood and took her hands in his. "Rosa, my dear, where did you come from?"

"The graveyard. Lydia and I were reading inscriptions." She giggled. "You know how I love history, Rob-ert." She pointed behind her. "Come on, let's explore."

As they wandered around the four acres of the walled-in cemetery, Rose stopped at one grave. "Oh, this child was only four years old." Her eyes darkened. "Her family's Catholic. I see them at the Cathedral all the time. I remember when she died a couple of years ago. So sad." She tightened the shawl around her shoulders.

Near a clear area, Rose took a quilt out of her bag, spread it close to the edge of an unused plot, and sat on it. Charles stood looking down and admiring her beauty.

Lydia hurried over with a basket. "Mr. Boyington, I hope you are hungry." The scent of fried chicken tempted his palate. She took out rolls and a salad, plus a container of tea, which she poured into glasses. Then she stepped back. "I will sit over there." She pointed to a gravesite in the corner shaded by a six-foot-tall live oak. Charles smiled as he sat beside Rose. "What a nice surprise."

He held up a drumstick. "Now don't tell me you cooked this, Rosa, my dear."

She shook her head. "I won't. Essie Mae, our slave, cooked everything, when Papa and Mama weren't around." She turned to face him. "I was in my room writing my journal, Charles, about the Leonid storm, showers of stars falling on Alabama. Can you believe 30,000 meteors fell per hour? Did you see it?"[6]

"I did. It was the day we landed in Mobile, November 3. A sight to behold."

"I know." Her eyes twinkled. "So was the way people reacted. Some fell on their knees, or pulled out dusty Bibles. Others threw dice and cards in the fire." She chuckled. "They thought it was the end of the world.'

"Except the Indians," Charles interjected. "They considered it a sign of good luck."[6] He leaned forward and gave her a peck on the cheek. "It certainly was a lucky day for me. It led to my meeting you, Rosa, my dear." He placed his arm around her shoulder and pulled her close, their lips almost touching.

"Oooh, we musn't, Charles." She pulled back but only a bit. "Lydia might look our way."

He drew her close again, and their eyes met. "I do not care, my love." He kissed her hard on the mouth, and she didn't resist.

If Lydia noticed, she didn't say a word. After the third kiss, Charles whispered in Rose's ear, "I'm seeing those stars right now, Rose, my dear, and they are beyond beautiful. It is like heaven."

"Moi, aussi, Charles. Moi, aussi."

FOUR

MERRY ? CHRISTMAS

Early Christmas morning, Charles stood at the washbasin and scrubbed his hands with lye soap until blood oozed from his thumbnail. Getting all the printer's ink from under his fingernails proved almost impossible. He then took a nail file and dug out extra residue. Studying his nails, he was pleased that they were cleaner than they'd been since he'd begun working for Pollard and Dade.

He left Nathaniel snoring and went to the outhouse, shivering on the way because the temperature had dropped. When he returned to his room, Nathaniel had gotten dressed. He sat on the edge of the bed, leaning over to tie his shoes. "I was going to look for you. We need to go to work." He coughed several times. "Where have you been?"

He handed Nathaniel a note. "I'm not going to work today. Please give this to Mr. Pollard."

"What? Christmas isn't a holiday, Charles."

"It is for me."

Nathaniel unfolded the note and read it. "This says you're sick, and you're not. You'd better watch out, Charles, you'll get fired. Where are you going today?"

"I've been invited to the de Fleur's for Christmas dinner." He took out a comb, stood at the mirror, and parted his hair in the middle. "I have to look my best."

"Oh, good gosh, Charles. You're only going to the de Fleur's, not to meet a king."

Charles whirled around. "Well, he is a baron." He squinted, "The story is told that he came to Demopolis, Alabama when the heroes—French expatriates—were granted land by Congress. It's called the Vine and Olive Colony. The stipulation was that they had to grow grapes and olives, but it failed. It's odd that Rose has never mentioned that."[1] He shrugged. "No matter, I want to make a good first impression. From all I've heard, he has a bad one of me now. I want to change that."

"Then bring him a bottle of good whiskey." Frost coughed again.

Reaching in a drawer, Charles pulled out a bag. "I've already thought of that, Nate."

"Aren't you going to gift wrap it?"

"What? No. A man doesn't care about frills." He slipped on the coat of the new suit he bought for the occasion. "I've got to go meet the florist and pick up some flowers for Mrs. de Fleur."

Frost took a deep breath. "What did you buy, Rose?"

Pulling a small, gift-wrapped box from his pocket, he held it up. "A necklace with a small pearl. I noticed she wears pearl earrings, and I tried to match them."

Nathaniel nodded. "Nice." He handed Charles some change. "Most stores will be open. Buy some wrapping paper. That whiskey looks really tacky in that old bag."

Charles took the change and left. But he pocketed it, and his only stop on the way to the de Fleur's was at the florist. On his six-block walk, children playing outside with new toys wished him well, and Charles returned their greetings. Laughter from open windows and doors lifted his spirits and his self-confidence as he made his way to face a formidable foe he hoped to turn into a friend, or at least to make the man *tolerate* him, even if only because of his daughter.

At the door of his hosts, Charles hesitated before knocking, but he vowed not to turn away. So, he rapped on the door three times.

Ellie cracked the door. "You Mr. Boyington?"

"Yes, I am."

She opened the door wide. "Come in, Suh. You expected." Without asking, she took the flowers and the bag and waited for dismissal.

Before he stepped across the hearth, Rose appeared. Charles spotted the mistletoe on the top of the doorframe, and when she came nearer, he gave her a quick peck on the cheek.

Ellie's hand flew to her mouth, covering a gasp. Then she took Charles" gifts and put them under a Christmas tree teeming with so much fruit, it must have taken at least a day to decorate it. But the chore probably fell to the slaves. Beneath it, as a reminder of the true meaning of Christmas, was a small hand-carved crèche with an angel on top.

Charles chuckled as Rose backed away from him. "A very happy Christmas, Rosa, my dear. And may there be many more."

Rose showed her snow-white teeth as she smiled. "And a wonderful Christmas to you, too, Charles." She motioned him to follow her but stopped short, saying, "Papa knows we've met at Mass, and he probably thinks you're Catholic. It will be best if you, uh, leave that impression."

Charles nodded, and followed her into a living room where her father sat in a huge, overstuffed chair. "Papa, may I present Mr. Charles Boyington?"

The Baron stood, held out his hand, and they shook. The Baron's firm grip relaxed as he withdrew his hand. He sized up Charles from head to toe. With lips barely parting, he said, "I see you're dressed for church but I don't recall seeing you at the Cathedral this morning."

"The church was very crowded." Charles hedged. Even in the thirteen by thirty-foot building, people jammed together at the doors could have prevented his being seen. He kept his gaze on his host. The Baron's similarity to his former leader surprised him. He had the demeanor of Napoleon, but he was much taller, and his face was more square. Charles halfway expected the Baron to slip his hand into his vest as Napoleon did. But he didn't, and his husky voice brought Charles back to the present.

"Of course the church was full; it's Christmas. I understand you're a printer. I'm surprised you did not have to work today." Staring at his guest, the Baron's lip curled into a sneer. "You dress well for a man of your means."

"Yessir. I did my apprenticeship in New Haven." His words made Charles glad he'd bought the Jackson coat of a green and Oxford mixed cloth and the ivory Florentine vest at St. John Price & Co., although it took most of his salary plus the money he'd received from his mother.[2]

"I see." The Baron raised his chin. "How long did that take; about two months?"

Charles squinted involuntarily. "No, Sir. About two years. You have to learn more than how to set type. I took lessons in grammar and…"

"Never mind the details." He walked away. "I hear a bell ringing. Dinner's ready."

No Christmas greeting, no interest in my work. Not a good start.

The Baron made a curt introduction to his wife who did honor him with a seasonal salutation: “Joyeux Noel, Mr. Boyington, and welcome to our home.” She cracked a smile which vanished the instant her husband frowned.

The Baron pointed to a chair. “Sit there.”

After they said grace, Ellie brought out serving plates of turkey, steaming vegetables and hot rolls topped with butter. She passed each one around. During the meal, both the Baron and Madame de Fleur ate without uttering a word.

“What did you get for Christmas?” Charles asked Rose, seated next to him.

“Oh, we don’t open gifts until after dinner.”

The Baron cleared his throat. “We don’t talk during dinner, Mr. Boyington, it’s not good for the digestion.”

Charles swallowed hard. His hand shook. He reached for a roll, tipped his wine glass and some spilled on the white linen tablecloth. “Sorry, Sir.” He dabbed at it with his napkin.

The Baron jerked the napkin away. “Please do not ruin the napkin, too.”

“Ellie,” he yelled, “Come here.”

Ellie rushed into the room, saw the problem, and hurried out. In less than a minute, she came back with a rag and dabbed it on the spot.

“Bring Mr. Boyington another napkin. But not one of the linen ones,” he ordered.

He turned to Charles. "Now, may we finish the meal in peace and silence, please? As I said, it's our custom not to talk while we're eating."

Charles nodded but didn't say a word. *It looks like you don't talk anytime. How did Rose come from a family like this? Maybe they're acting this way just because I'm here. God, I've made things worse, not better.*

After a dessert of apple and pecan pie, the Baron announced, "We'll now go into the living room and open the gifts." He led the parade with Charles at the rear.

The Baron received a pipe, some shirts, and a couple of books. Madame de Fleur unwrapped gifts of a diamond bracelet, a scarf, and slippers. Rose ooed and awed over a dress, a hat full of feathers in a hatbox, and a handbag. Three gifts each. Next, Charles pointed to the flowers. "Those are for you, Mrs. de Fleur." Then he reached over and handed the bottle of whiskey to the Baron. "And for you."

The Baron peeked into the bag and glanced at the label. "I only drink Scotch." He took the bottle back to the kitchen. "My slaves may appreciate it."

Madame de Fleur said, "Thank you. The flowers are lovely." She handed Charles a wrapped gift. "My husband bought this for you." Then she followed her husband out of the room.

Charles pulled Rose's gift from his pocket and handed it to her. "I hope you like this."

She tore it open, took out the necklace, gave him a peck on the cheek, "I love it, Charles; it's beautiful." She shoved a curl behind her ear. "It matches my earrings." She put it around her neck and had him fasten it. "Don't pay attention to Papa. I told you he treats all my suitors that way."

Charles shook his head side to side. "I made things worse. I shouldn't have come here."

"Oh, no. Papa did give you a gift." She gave the package to him. "Open it."

Tearing off the wrapper, he stared at the book before him. The title made him blink. *Etiquette for Those Seeking Success.*

Stuffing the book under his arm, he avoided letting Rose see the title. But enough was enough. He couldn't stand one more minute of insults. "I must leave, Rosa, my dear." He took her hand in his. "But I refuse to stop seeing you. I'll send you a note, and we'll meet—no matter what your father says." Footsteps alerted him that the Baron was returning to the living room. He threw Rose a kiss as he slipped out the door.

As soon as he was out of sight, he dropped to the ground and did something he hadn't done since he was ten years old. His face fell into cupped hands, and he blinked back tears. Raising his head, he cried out loud. *What a hell of a Christmas. It was anything except Merry!*

FIVE

KNOW WHEN TO FOLD THEM

Wending his way to Stony's, Charles headed for the back room. The girl who opened a door had sugar in her voice as she leaned close to him. "Well, hel-lo, Mr. Boyington, you're mighty dressed up tonight, aren't you?" She fingered the sleeve of his coat. "Nice."

He brushed her hand aside. "Not in the mood, Lizzy."

She shrugged. "Fine with me." Backing off, she let him pass.

Three men sat around a maple poker table bearing chipped edges from overuse. They grumbled without looking up from their hands of cards. "Pull up a chair." Frog said in his guttural voice. "We need another sucker to bleed."

Charles looked around. Frog had the only familiar face.

"This here's Fred and Arnie." Frog made the informal introduction. "Ante's a dollar, minimum's a dollar; maximum's ten."

Charles removed his coat and placed it on the back of the chair. He took out a silver dollar and put it in front of him. He left ten ones in his pocket; if the stakes hit the maximum, he only had enough for one hand.

The door flung open, and Tommy John stormed in. "Sorry I'm late." He clutched Charles's shoulder and cringed at the cigar smoke fouling up the air. "Well, look who's here! Haven't seen you for a couple of weeks. I reckon you been busy with little Rose, right? It's Christmas night; how come you're not with her now?"

Charles cocked his head. "How'd you know I even met Rose?"

"Har, har." Tommy John plopped into a chair next to Charles. "Mobile ain't nothin' but a small town. Word gets around. Besides, I saw you dancing with her at the Alabama Hotel. Wasn't hard to tell you were smitten with her." He squinted. "By the way, why'd you leave the ball so early? I had plans to introduce you to some influential people."

Damn. I should have stayed longer at that ball. Yeah. I was so awed with Rose that I let my goal pass by. I don't usually do that. But I just wasn't focused. He's right; I was, I am, "smitten" with Rose, and maybe more than that. I think I'm in love.

Tommy John laid his hand on Charles' sleeve. "Hey, boy, what's the matter? You didn't answer my question." He rubbed the material. "Man, that's some fancy shirt, silk, ain't it? You got some money we don't know about? Some kinda job on the side?"

Charles chuckled. He chose to answer Tommy John's last question and ignore the other two. "No, I don't have any extra jobs," he growled. "As for the money, deal me in and let's see if I can make some more." He sat and snapped his fingers. "Let's get on with the game."

"What's the matter with you, boy?" Tommy John glared at him. "You usually act more friendly. Girl trouble?"

"None of your damn business! Deal."

"Okay. Forget it." Tommy John slid the deck of cards to Arnie who dealt the hands.

Tommy John won the first hand of five-card stud with two pairs, aces and sevens. The second hand he won with a pair of kings. When he said, “Gotcha, boy,” to Charles, he didn’t receive a reply.

After Charles lost two hands, he shoved his next bet to the center of the table.

Tommy John glared at him. “Don’t you know better than to splash the pot?” He pushed a pile of dollar bills back in front of Charles. “Only the dealer can do that. Where’s your mind tonight, Boy?”

Charles rubbed his chin. “Oh, my luck’s running bad. But it’s got to change. Can you stake me for, uh, three hundred, Tommy John? I want to stay in the game.”

Tommy John scratched his head. “Well, poker’s a new game, only been around about three years, and it looks like you learned it pretty well. You’ve recouped before. I reckon it’s worth a chance.” Pulling out a roll of money, he counted out three hundred in twenties, tens, and ones. “You damn well better hope your luck changes, Charles. And you better be good for this.”

For three hours, Charles sat at the table losing money, drinking beer, and munching on crackers and cheese while watching his partners rake in dollar bills time after time. He kept thinking of the baron’s snubbing and insults. Worse yet, he wondered how he’d manage to see Rose despite her arrogant father’s dislike of him and his attitude toward his job as a lowly printer. Her mother seemed nice enough, but subject to her husband’s will. The Baron controlled the family. But he didn’t control Rose. No. She was an intelligent person. She’d make her own decisions—wouldn’t she?

“Hey, Boyington, I asked you twice. Are you in or not?” Tommy John blurted out. “Hell, pay attention!”

Charles looked at the space in front of him. All of his money was gone. He turned to Tommy John. "Can you stake me for another couple of hands; give me a chance to win it back?"

Lips pressed together, Tommy John nodded, pulled two fives and ten ones out of his pocket, and glared at the man sitting beside him. "You better pray you win now, or you better find a damn good way to pay up."

Twenty minutes later, Charles was in deeper than before. He shoved his chair back and said, "I'm out." He bit the corner of his lip. Then it hit him that he'd lost more money than he intended, much more. "Look, Tommy John, I'm, uh, it'll take me a little time to cover my loss, but I'm good for it."

"You better be," Tommy John replied.

"Don't worry." Charles slipped on his jacket. "I'll get it." He gritted his teeth. *I should have known when to fold my hands. Now what? How can I get out of this?*

Tommy John pointed to Charles' coat. "You may need to sell that. I'm not plannin' to wait long. *When* will you get it and pay off?"

"I get paid Saturday."

"Har, har. Don't bluff. Ain't no printer gets paid that much. I kept track; you owe me three hundred dollars and twenty dollars." Tommy John stood facing Charles, almost a head taller than he was. More muscular than he looked seated, too. "You better learn when to fold 'em."

I need to get out of here and figure this out. Men like Tommy John won't wait for their money. He backed away slowly, holding up a palm. "I've played with you before. You know I'm good for it. Hey, give me a chance tomorrow night, and I might win it all back. What do you say?"

Tommy John took charge. “Okay, son. You be here then, and we’ll see what happens. Just remember, if you lose more, you’ll just be in bigger trouble.” He scratched his chin. “I bet you know we kinda count on you losing. But if you expect to win, you’d best forget that little lady and come with your head on straight. Win or lose, you also better have a plan. All you get is one day’s grace; Then you better have a way to pay. We got plans, and we got people to enforce them. Get it?”

Shaken by those words, Charles left. As soon as he reached the street, he ran. Out of breath by the time he reached the boarding house, Charles slowed to a walk. He needed a few minutes to conjure up a reason to ask his roommate for a loan, a big one. And he had to use his talent as a wordsmith and calmly present his case to sound convincing. Now focused and back in control, he entered the boarding house, walked down the hall, and took a deep breath before going into his room and awakening Nate to make his request. This couldn’t wait.

SIX

COURTING ROSE

Almost every weekday, Charles enjoyed sitting next to his sweetheart at Mass. Once in a while, when Rose's mother also attended, Lydia would sit between them. The words of the liturgy and the sermon never registered; Charles was too busy thinking of lines of poetry he'd write to his lover.

A couple of days after the Christmas fiasco with Rose's father, he met her at the Cathedral's early morning Mass and handed a note to Lydia for Rose, saying, "Rosa, my dear, I want to ring in the New Year with you at my side. I've finagled an invitation to the New Year's Eve Ball at the Alabama Hotel. Could you meet me there? We can sneak away and watch the fireworks on the wharf to greet the New Year. I will be at Mass tomorrow, and I await your reply."

The next morning, as Charles eased into the pew five minutes after Mass started, Rose placed her shoulder close to his and handed him a note. "Yes, dear Robert, I will be at the ball. I have good news: Lydia has agreed to let us escape as you suggested. She will be watching, but not too closely."

When he turned to her and smiled, she winked at him.

Almost every day that week, Charles enjoyed sitting next to his sweetheart at Mass. One day, since Rose's mother was there, Lydia sat between them. Once again, the priest's words didn't register; Charles wrote poetry in his head to his lover and anticipated their New Year's Eve meeting.

Eighteen hundred and thirty-four came in with a literal bang, not from the fireworks but from a storm. It lit the sky with lightning syncopated by roars of thunder. City officials canceled the fireworks' display. Charles and Rose didn't let the inclement weather or the lack of entertainment interfere with their pleasure. They danced the night away while Lydia stood on the sidelines.

Horns blew at midnight, but partygoers stayed inside. Charles kissed his love and pecked Lydia on the cheek. His "Happy New Year" was met by the same greeting from Rose.

"Our plans were thwarted a bit by the weather, Rosa, my dear," he whispered in her ear, "but I have bigger ones. I'm taking a day off Friday. I'll meet you at the Cathedral, and we'll spend the day at our secret place."

Rose cocked her head. "You mean the Church Street Graveyard?"

"Ah, no, my sweet, I mean in the woods we visited, you remember, don't you? Our first real kiss. Where Mr. Roper is building his plantation home." He squeezed her hand. "I have something to give you."

Her eyes widened. "What is it?"

"It's a secret."

"Now you have me wondering, please tell me what it is, Charles. Pretty please."

"That would spoil the surprise." He shook his finger at her. "Actually, I have two gifts."

"Charles Rob-ert! You've made me more curious than ever. I don't think I can wait until Friday."

But she had to. Charles refused to concede and reveal his secret gifts.

On Friday, when they reached the woodsy spot, the mansion's construction had progressed considerably, but the grounds in front remained in pristine condition. Except for tracks made by workmen, it was virtually untouched. Lydia spread a large quilt on the ground, and Charles and Rose sat on it.

Pulling a thermos and cups from a picnic basket, Lydia said, "I brought biscuits, too, but they're barely warm." When she reached into her bag and took out a linen napkin, Charles winced. *Looks like the one I spilled wine on, but it's clean.* Unfolding it, Lydia revealed its contents—three biscuits.

Charles handed one to Rose and then took a bite of another. "Mmm, this is delicious, wonderful blueberry jam. Did you make these, Lydia."

"Oh, no. I don't do any of the cooking. Ellie and her mama take care of that. Her mama made these. She is a good cook, isn't she?"

With mouths full, both Charles and Rose nodded.

Lydia rose. "I think I'll go take a look at the house." She pointed in its direction. "From here, it looks like a little Greek Temple. As it is when viewing a forest, a broad view is different. Amid the trees, you miss that. The house, too, will look different up close."

"Well," Rose said, "maybe that's good. People are interested in Greek culture all over the western world, Lydia. They're learning Greek in school, and democracy flourished in Greece."

She turned to Charles. "Have you learned that, around here, people often give their homes romantic names. *Leigh* means meadow, so *Oakleigh* is appropriate for this one. All thirty-three acres are full of oaks, and it looks like a meadow."

Lydia waved. “Goodbye. You two enjoy yourselves. Don’t worry, I won’t give the workmen a hint you’re here.” Her lip curled into a half smile as she wandered away without glancing back.

As soon as Lydia was out of sight, Charles reached into his pocket, opened a small box, and took out a sheet of paper. He unfolded the paper and read:

No. 1

A SKETCH—A FRAGMENT

They met—ot in the city’s busy throng,

Of thousands, where the mingled mass along

The soilless streets, on business each intent,

Pass heedlessly,--but where meandering bent,

With graceful curves, the crystal mirror’d brook,

And where, fanned by the sighing zephyrs, shook

The foliage round, of flowers of varied hues

And gentle herbage, whereupon the dews

Of eve sat glistening in the moon’s bright way.

As forth, on high, she held her star-lit way,

’T was there—silent yet eloquent they met—

Silent, for on each quiv’ring lip was set

The seal of modest love; yet eloquent,

For each alternate spoke, as doth, when bent

Upon the dearly lov’d, the lover’s eye,

As doth the warm-pressed hand and broken sigh

Speak love’s and nature’s language, as doth speak

Boyington Oak: A Grave Injustice

The ashy, pale and blood suffused check.

It was signed *Mobile, Feb., 1833* *AEOLIAN.*[1]

When he finished, Rose looked at him doe-eyed. "Ah, that's lovely. And you wrote it just for me? How sweet."

He held up his palm. "I'd do anything for you, my love, and I'm not finished." He handed her the box. In the center was a miniature heart, painted red on the front and *Rosa, my dear, I love you* was etched in tiny letters on the back. "I made this for you, too. My friend, Nathaniel, showed me how to carve it."

Rose hopped into his lap and gave him a long kiss. "Ah, Charles Robert, I love it. And you, too, you don't know how much." Her face glowed as she re-wrapped the heart in layers of tissue paper and slipped it into the neckline of her dress. "I have a chain to put it on, and I'll wear it always, dear Charles. It will remind me you are my one true love. It will tie us together, and we'll never really be apart."

Charles leaned back and raised his brows. "What about your father?"

"Oh, dear Rob-ert," she took his hand into hers., "even my father can't keep us apart. Don't worry, I can convince him you're worthy of my love." A passionate kiss, followed by many more, sealed the compact.

An hour later, Lydia announced her return from a few yards away. "Yoo, hoo. Are you two ready for lunch?" Upon arrival at the site, she, picked up the picnic basket, took out a tablecloth, and spread it on the ground. Without looking in Rose and Charles' direction, she said, "Oh, you ought to see that house. It's magnificent, all that I expected, and more."

But the two lovers weren't interested. Busy looking into each other's eyes, they didn't respond to Lydia's raving about Oakleigh's beauty. Neither budged until Lydia gasped in a loud whisper. "Oh, dear God, hurry up and grab everything; we need to leave here fast."

SEVEN

CONFRONTATION

They didn't escape fast enough. Hurrying down the path worn by workers, the three stopped short of the clearing opening to the road. Facing them was the Baron flanked by Ellie with her teeth chattering, and a tall, lanky slave Rose recognized as Lazarus, their groundskeeper. He had a tight grip on the shovel in his hand.

The three stopped short. "Just where have you been, young lady?" Baron de Fleur growled through gritted teeth.

Rose lifted her chin. "We've been on a picnic, Papa." Her voice was strong and firm.

The Baron took a step forward, within inches of his daughter's face. "You know that's NOT what I mean. Now tell me the truth. What have you been doing here in these woods?" His two guards moved up to resume their places at his side.

"Papa," Rose blurted out, "I am a grown woman, not a child. I shouldn't have to account to you for my every move."

Wide-eyed, her father sputtered, "Pfaff, if you live in my house, you do. Read the Bible."

"I do read the Bible, Papa." She squared her shoulders. "And I go to church more often than you. I never miss a Sunday Mass, either."

"Harrumph! Does that give you the right to be insolent? Are you ready to leave my home? Perhaps this *printer"*—he acknowledged Charles's presence for the first time—"can provide for you in a manner to which you are *not* accustomed." He folded his arms. "Would lowering your class and your standards of living appeal to you?"

Rose stared straight into the Baron's eyes. "You may be my father, but I don't know you."

Turning to Charles, she said, "Let's go."

Charles followed her as she made a semi-circle around the Baron and his guards. Ellie gave her arm a pat as she passed to make her way onto the road beyond.

The Baron didn't try to stop her, but he grabbed Lydia's arm. "You're going with me, and you'll tell me everything I want to know." He glared at her. "And I mean everything."

#

"I feel bad about getting Lydia in trouble," Rose said when they reached Government Street, removed from her father's wrath. "Maybe we should go back and try to help her."

"No, that would only raise your Papa's ire," Charles retorted.

"I guess you're right. The best thing I can do is go home and talk to Mama. She'll understand, but I doubt that she'll cross Papa. Woe is me."

"I'll go with you."

"No, that wouldn't help." They were within a block of her house. She kissed her lover. "You go home. I'd rather speak to her alone." She looked around. "I'd better hurry. I don't want Papa to beat me home."

A few minutes later, Rose walked into her home. In Ellie's absence, her mother opened the door. "Where have you been all day, Rose? We were worried. Papa's gone out looking for you."

"I'm fine." She gave her mother a hug. "To tell you the truth, I've been with Charles over by the Roper house in the woods…"

"In the woods?" Her mother's folded hands shook.

"Don't worry. Lydia was with us." She didn't adhere to the whole truth.

"Did Papa find you?"

Rose nodded. "Yes, he did and he made a terrible scene. He threatened to make me leave *his* house, as he called it."

"Oh, dear, oh good gracious. He must have been very angry." She blinked several times. "Why, what…" She pulled her daughter close, then backed away, squaring her shoulders. "Well, that just isn't going to happen!"

The Baron slung the front door open and stormed into the house.

"Go to your room, Rose!" He screeched. "I'll take care of this. Shoo."

Stomping into the living room, the Baron faced his wife. "I found your daughter. She'd been way out in the woods near the house Roper's building, with that Yankee printer. Do you know he's a gambler, too? Do you? He has debts he can't pay. Le clochard!"

He cursed in French and kept raving without waiting for an answer. "He frequents the red-light district. Lord knows what other company he keeps."[1] He banged his fist on a table so hard it shook, and a cut glass candy dish fell to the floor, breaking into four pieces. Ellie hurried into the room and cleaned it up without saying a word.

"Get out of here, Ellie," the Baron screamed at her although she'd already scurried out of the room and didn't reply.

When she saw her daughter peeking through the door, Mrs. de Fleur spoke up. "*Our* daughter will not be put out of our home. I've spoken with her. Lydia was with them. Nothing was wrong, Baron. Where is Lydia now? Call her in here and she'll verify what Rose told me."

"What! I'll do no such thing. My dear wife, don't question my decisions. I am in charge of this house." He glared at the woman facing him. "This is so unlike you. Have you lost your mind?"

She took a deep breath. "No, for once, I think I've found it. When it comes to Rose, from now on, I plan to take charge of decisions. You will *not* make her leave this house."

As the Baron yelled out, "What has come over you?" to his wife and hustled out of the room, his gait faltered, and he stumbled on the edge of the rug and cursed aloud.

When his wife yelled back, "Vous etes un fou!" he turned and glared at her; this time she glared back. The Baron threw up his hands and left the room.

Rose turned to Ellie and giggled. "What a surprise. She called Father a fool. I didn't know Mama had such spunk."

"Lordy, Miss Rose, peoples can come up with lotsa courage when it comes to they chile, can't they?"

"Yes, Ellie, we defend the ones we love at great risk."

How this would relate to Charles, Rose had yet to determine. One thing she knew: her father was wrong; being a printer was not a lowly job; it required intelligence to make it through the apprenticeship. Rose also knew love overcomes worse obstacles than changing social or economic status. She could adapt to her lover's circumstances.

EIGHT

LOST JOB

But Charles's career as a printer ended. When he lost his job, his circumstances changed drastically.

"Damn it. I'm not the one who should have been laid off," Charles grumbled as he headed for his destination. Recently installed gaslights provided illumination on North Royal Street as the printer made his way toward Pollard and Dade Printing Company, his former employers.

A horse-drawn carriage rushed past, causing Boyington to step sideways to avoid it and the splashing mud. He shook his fist at the driver. "Watch where you're going!" After checking his tailor-made black suit and finding it untouched, he hurried along.

Printers were working late that evening to complete a job, one they were glad to have, but they wouldn't be open much longer. Business had decreased, and Boyington had been laid off. One report said it was because he spent too much time writing poetry. Others blamed it on his often being late for work.

Mulling over multiple problems, he took long strides. In addition to his gambling debts, his room and board were due. He needed to pick up his last salary.

When the shop came into view, he saw a crowd gathered at the front door and two men carrying another to the carriage that had passed him. He rushed forward calling out, "What's the problem?"

His question was answered when he saw the man in trouble. "Nate, my friend, did you have another spell?" he asked his roommate.

The pale-faced printer nodded from his supine position. "Yes, Charles, it's the consumption. They're taking me to the hospital."

Charles edged closer and grabbed his hand. "I'll go with you."

Turning to Pollard, he said, "Could I get my pay, please?"

Pollard nodded, went into his office, returned with an envelope, and handed it to Boyington without a word.

Boyington got into the carriage beside Frost, his sad-faced friend, and it bounced forward as the horses trotted away. He counted the money—twelve dollars and fifty cents—and slipped it into his empty wallet. "I need this. I lost a little last night…"

Frost raised his head and whispered in a shaky voice, "Charles, you know you can't beat the odds at Stony's, or any other place. Why don't you quit gambling?"

Boyington's lips formed a straight line. "It's my money. You can't…" he noticed Frost's face becoming even whiter and held up his hand. "This is no time to discuss that. Lay back down, Natee." He forced a smile. "You're sick, and you need to stay calm."

When they reached Mobile City Hospital, a Sister of Charity wearing a white, ankle-length habit and a huge white headpiece looking like a bird on the wing greeted them. "You're in our hands and God's now, Mr. Frost." She smiled at the patient as she adjusted the rosary with large beads hanging from the sash on her waist. "We'll take good care of you and you'll be fine."

"Please do what you can for him," Boyington said.

Turning to Boyington who stepped across the pile of dirty rags on the floor to come closer, she whispered, "I'm only here temporarily to help out. This hospital has so many patients and so few staff. One in four deaths is due to consumption." She shrugged. "About all we can do is keep them away from others and make them as comfortable as possible, until, uh, until they die." She blinked back tears.

"Thank you." Boyington waved goodbye as they wheeled his friend away on a gurney; his slim body looked frailer than usual, and his shirt hung loose on his shrunken shoulders. He managed a two-finger wave as he passed.

Boyington tuned to the carriage driver. "Take me home, please. It's Captain George's Boarding House. Include my fare in the bill you send my friend." He climbed into the carriage, leaned against the headrest, and closed his eyes. In a sleepy voice, he told the driver, "Pick me up tomorrow afternoon at one forty-five. Visiting hours start at two p.m."

"They have morning visiting hours at eleven a.m., Sir."

"I know." Charles yawned.

When they reached the boarding house, Charles climbed the wide steps onto the porch that made a semi-circle on the front and side of the clapboard house. It was built on concrete piers as a protection from the rising water of Mobile River only two blocks to the East. Peering into the floor to ceiling windows, he made sure nobody was around. Because of overdue rent, he wanted to avoid a confrontation with the landlord. He entered the unlocked front door, stepped into the parlor lit by a smelly kerosene lamp hanging on the wall, and tiptoed down the center hall of the home's dogtrot design, stopping before reaching the back door. Using a skeleton key, he unlocked the door to his room and entered.

Inside, Charles tossed his hat and coat on a coat rack. He took out a packet of matches and lit a candle on a table between two single beds. Light flickered off the cracked plaster of the cream-colored ceiling. He pulled a straight-backed chair up to a mahogany kneehole desk that also served as a dresser shared by the two men. He had three drawers, and Nathaniel used the other three. After moving the candle to the desktop, he reached into the top drawer on his side and retrieved a pencil and a pad of paper he'd sneaked out of the print shop. On the top of the ruled paper, he jotted down a budget.

He wrote, *$12.50 – Pay $3.50 toward rent – Keep $5.00 for food - Bet $4.00 on horse race - Parlay into $25.00 – Pay Nate $20.00 - Keep gambling - From winnings, Pay Nat. $50 of $100 – Don't pay Tommy John - leave Mobile—can do—have skipped out on debts before. Nobody's going to catch up with me.*

He stood and stretched. He stuffed the paper into the back pocket of his pants and pulled out a key. Removing his clothes, he placed them in the second drawer, got out a flannel nightshirt, and slipped into it. He took a box from the desk, unlocked it, and dumped the contents on the desktop. Pulling out a journal, he read: "I've worn out my welcome with George Williamson. Found another printer to room with—Nathaniel Frost." He smirked. "Old Nate's wrong. The hell with what they say about the house always coming out on top. If I just keep playing, I can win."

From the center of the pile, he retrieved a dog-eared news clip, unfolded it, and read the headlines: HORSE THIEF APPREHENDED,[1] "But they didn't keep me long. I'm fairly safe here. The only problem in a town like Mobile with 3,190 residents is that everybody knows each other sooner or later. But I haven't been here long enough to become well known."

He cracked a smile. "People who do know me are society folks. They'd have the influence to help me. And I think I've gained their trust. Besides, all they have in Mobile is a volunteer police force."[2] He chuckled as he placed the news clip back in the box along with the other contents. “In this town, I could probably get away with murder.”

NINE

DISRUPTION OF LIFE

The next day, Charles awakened from a dream about his dismissal. He relived that Monday when he showed up for work at 8:15 a.m. at Pollard and Dade Print Shop and was called into the office.

"Sorry I'm late," he announced. "I did not awaken on time."

Mr. Pollard looked up from his roll-top desk. "Mr. Boyington," he said, "I regret to inform you that your services are no longer required."

Charles stood at attention. "I won't be late again, Mr. Pollard; I can promise you that. You see, I've been up at night helping Mr. Frost, and…"

Pollard held up his palm. "That's not the only problem. Our business has fallen off, and we simply cannot afford to keep you employed."[1]

"But, Mr. Pollard, I need the job. Perhaps I could solicit some business. I have contacts in Mobile. In fact, I am, uh, friends with Baron de Fleur, perhaps I could convince him to send some customers here."

Pollard's eyes widened. "I don't think the Baron is in need of our services. He's retired."

"But he has contacts," Boyington persisted.

"Perhaps, but one or two new accounts won't take up the slack, Boyington. Our business has slowed down considerably."

"Well, could I work part-time? Even that would help me out."

"I'm afraid not. We can barely afford to keep Mr. Frost employed part-time." Pollard shoved his chair back and stood. "If things improve, I can get in touch with you."

Charles awakened, wondering if things would improve. He wrote a letter to Rose telling her he'd lost his job and thinking of leaving the South, but he said, "I cannot entertain the thought of leaving you…I cannot ask you to be my wife until I get back to work again" Dated April 25, 1834, and signed ROBERT.[2]

Gloom and melancholy took over. *What next? How can I survive with no income?* This situation left him no choice. Why he was let go and Frost kept his job didn't seem fair. *I'm the better printer with more experience. And I'm healthier than Nate. He's sick. He may not even survive too long. Then what will Pollard and Dale do? Hmm, maybe they'll rehire me. Maybe not; their decisions aren't logical.* Their choice to fire him didn't make sense.

But that was no longer Charles's problem. Survival was. He had written Frost a letter asking for help saying:

Dear Mr. Frost,

> *I have a confession to make as usual. I am in need of some money, not a large amount, but enough to do me until next Sunday, and to pay the slave woman for my washing. I expect some money from back home, and I will return the amount immediately on the arrival of the packet*
>
> *Mobile, April 10, 1834*
>
> *BOYINGTON*[3]

But the formal request brought no response. Charles had eyed his friend's gold watch. It was expensive. He knew Nate also had an alternate source of income from an inheritance. A sizeable one. This might be a good time to capitalize on that. Maybe he should jog his friend's memory. He'd helped Nate and been paid for it. Now, he'd have to do more and be paid better. He raised his eyes to the sky. *There's always a way to solve a problem. And I know how to find it.*

TEN

SURVIVAL

The next day, released from the hospital, Nathaniel invited Charles to take a walk with him, saying, “The fresh air is good for both of us.”

As they headed to the Church Street Graveyard, Nathaniel straightened his stooped shoulders as much as he could. He took Charles’ arm. “Look, my friend,” he said in a shaky voice. “I, uh, well, I feel terrible that you were, uh, let go, and I was retained.” He sighed. “You have more experience as a printer than I do.”

“I wouldn’t say that, Nate.” *But I really am. What is he leading up to?* “You’re lucky to keep your job. It is ironic, though, that *you’re* sick but *I* get the boot. Life’s not fair.”

“I know how you feel. You’ve helped me so much Charles. I treasure your assistance and your friendship. I’m not a rich man; so, I can’t repay you fully, but I want to do what I can.” He reached into his pocket, pulled out a bill, and squinted. “My eyesight’s getting worse. I need to get some of those new-fangled pince-nez glasses.” He stuffed a five-dollar bill in Charles' hand. “Take this. There’s more where that comes from. I’ll increase what I’ve been giving you every week.”

“No, I can’t take your money,” Charles said, but his head involuntarily bobbed up and down in a nod, and he kept his grip on the bill. *He saved me the trouble of asking for money. Maybe my luck is changing.* His brain clicked. *He says there’s more? I bet I know where it is.*

As they walked together, Charles let Nate ramble on about the flowers and the inscriptions on the graves large enough to read. But he didn't pay attention to what Nate said, his mind was on checking on the money, planning what he could do, and relishing the anticipation of staking quite a few poker games with his loot. Using his poker skills, he could multiply Nate's money many times.

When they arrived back at the boarding house, Mrs. George said, "You have some mail, Charles," and she took an envelope from her apron pocket and handed it to him.

The return address said it was from Connecticut. Charles knew who sent it. He'd appealed to his family for assistance for the fourth time, and his brother, who was a minister, sent a reply. While Nathaniel sat down to the supper table, Charles took the letter to his room.

My Dear Brother,

I am sorry to hear of your unfortunate circumstances. I know it's discouraging to lose your job, but keep trying and you will find another one. God provides.

My congregation is growing but it is small and my parishioners are not rich. The collections barely cover our expenses and my salary is not a large one. This is the last time I will be able to assist you. I am enclosing what I can in hopes that it will tide you over. Please use it for your boarding house bills and food needs.

Charles snatched up the five-dollar-bill that was enclosed, threw down the letter, and sat on his bed, glaring at it. "Damn. He's making a slur about my gambling," he muttered through clenched teeth. "Can't he realize I survive by my wits?"

He picked it up and read the rest.

Mother doesn't have any more money to give you, but she sends all of her love and says she will write soon. She always keeps you in her prayers.

Take care and keep the faith.

Your loving brother.

Edwin

Charles sucked in his breath. "Cheapskate! He's cutting me off. Looks like my mother is, too. She didn't even enclose a note this time. I guess she's given up on me." He stuck the bill in his pocket and stood.

"Well, Nathaniel, my dear chum, things have narrowed down to you and me." He stared at the floor, got up, and walked across the room. Lifting a tattered throw rug, he pulled out a box. With a pocketknife, he managed to pry open the lock. Then he took a few musty bills from a stack paper-clipped together. Scribbling an IOU for a hundred dollars, he stuffed it underneath the bills, replaced the paper clip, re-locked the box, and put back the rug.

"All right, dear brother, I'll use this stash and triple it, or more. Then I'll repay you your measly five bucks, and I'll pay Nate back, too. You'll see how living by my wits pays off."

Strutting into the dining room, Charles took his place at the table. "Good evening, everyone. How are you all?" He helped himself to a large chicken breast, rice, gravy, green beans, and a roll. "Ah, everything looks good. Nathaniel and I had an invigorating walk, and I am hungry. Besides, I need energy. Tomorrow, I will be busy interviewing for a job." He didn't bother to say he had no appointments with prospective employers.

He turned to Mrs. George, who collected the rent, "Madam, I will see you after dinner to pay my rent for this month—and the next." Then he focused on his food with thoughts of the poker game he now had funds to play. He'd head there right after this meal.

Twenty minutes later, Charles handed Mrs. George rent money, excused himself, slipped on a jacket, and left for Stoney's. Ten minutes afterward, he walked through the bar to the smoke-filled room where Frog sat alone puffing on a cigar.

"Ain't nobody here yet, Charlie." Frog narrowed his eyes. "You got a job? You got money? I heard you're in big debt to some of these guys. They ain't gonna let you play before you pay up."

Charles waved a couple of ten-dollar bills. "They'll let me play when I show them this. They know I'm good for my debt, and they'll give me a chance to win some money back." He raised his chin. "I might be young, Frog, but I've been around. Poker's new, but it's my game. I've got a knack for it, and these guys like the challenge."

"Humph. Sonny, you ain't been around near as long as I have. Better watch your step, or you'll get in so deep you'll neva get out. You're dealin' with a tough bunch." He pointed to the door. "Here they come now."

Charles won the first three games, then started losing. When he had doubled his former debt, he folded. "I'm out of here." Standing to face glares, he held up his palm. "I'm good for it. Give me five days. My friend will help me out."

Silence provoked him to say, "You don't know this, but my brother is a minister. I'll get the money from him if I have to."

Frog stared at him. "I warned you."

Backing out the door, insisting, "I'm good for it. I'll pay up," Charles let it slam behind him. He took huge strides until he left the building. He ran toward the boarding house, looking over his shoulder every few minutes. When Charles entered the hallway and tiptoed to his room, he was relieved nobody had followed him.

Since he found his roommate sound asleep in his bed, Charles considered raiding the money-box again but thought better of it. What would happen if Nate awakened? What could he say? What excuse would he have? None. No, that would be too risky.

He undressed, slipped on his nightclothes, and crawled into bed, pulling the cover over his head. By the light of a single candle sending out flickers that illuminated the wall, he contemplated his precarious situation.

His gambling debt had risen to four figures. He didn't have anywhere near that kind of money or any potential to get it. He didn't even have a job. If he took much more from Nate's stash, even with his bad eyesight, Nate might discover it was missing. He could show Nate the IOU's as proof that he intended to pay it back. But how? He had to admit he'd drained his mother and his brother dry. Now, it was unlikely his cohorts would let him play any more poker. Unless he found a new game.

He sat up in bed. A new game. That was it! A new chance to win. A change of luck. He blew out the candle.

But before he went to sleep, two disturbing thoughts forced themselves into his mind: Frog's words, "I warned you," and the more unnerving possibility that if Rose's father found out about his debts, he'd be more adamant about keeping them apart.

When Charles said aloud, "Oh, Rosa, My Dear, I can't live without you," Nate stirred.

"What's that, Charles?" Nate slurred.

"Nothing, Nate, go back to sleep."

He did, but Charles couldn't put Rose out of his mind. Between longing for her and the fear of what retribution those gamblers might seek, he tossed and turned until the wee hours of the morning.

ELEVEN

BACKLASH

Charles could put off creditors from clothing stores who sent overdue bills, and he managed to stall when his next rent came due, but he had to stay away from the poker games because of being in deep debt to other gamblers. He knew they had no qualms about getting their money any way they could. If they couldn't, his body might be found in a back alley off Theater Street or out in the woods near Oakleigh. Or they might beat him and break his bones, leaving him a cripple. Either way, their backlash would be relentless.

He'd also begged all he could from friends up north. Word got around New Haven that no loans to Charles were being repaid, and that cash flow came to a halt. When it reached the point that he dare not leave the boarding house even to meet Rose, he tried another appeal to his mother.

This time, his mother replied, *Thank you so much for your letter. It touched my heart, and I cried when I read it. It distresses me to see you in need. You express your feelings so eloquently, Charles. I'd help you if I could, Son, but I must help your brother, too. I don't have anything left. I'm so sorry.*

I am so looking forward to seeing you again. I do hope you can still arrange to meet in June at the residence of your brother.

With all my love,

Mother

How did she think he could afford a trip to New York? That would require leaving Mobile with debts unpaid, and finding a way to beg, borrow, or steal the money to finance the trip.[1] Charles still wanted to see his mother, so he wouldn't give up on the trip. But he had reached his limits. He was desperate to the point of wondering where his next meal would come from. So he ate more than usual.

At the dinner table Saturday, when Charles took a second chicken breast, George slammed his fist on the table. "That's enough, Charles." He snatched the serving fork from his boarder's hand. "You don't pay your damned room and board, and you eat twice as much as any of us." He dropped the chicken back on the serving platter. "I'm not running a charity house." He motioned toward the door with his thumb. "Get out. Go back to your room and pack—if you have anything to pack. You're evicted."

Wide-eyed, Nathaniel Frost raised his frail body to a standing position. In a shaky voice, he said, "Just a minute, Mr. George. You can't do that. Charles has no place to go." He pointed to Charles now braced against the door where he'd stopped before entering the hallway.

George stood, shoving his chair aside. "Oh, yes, I can." His booming voice echoed around the room. "I can evict anybody who doesn't pay their damn rent…"

Frost reached into his pocket and pulled out a couple of bills. "Here." He handed them to William George. "That should take care of it."

George cleared his throat. "All right," he said as he sat back in his chair.

He wagged a finger at Charles. "But don't expect to be late again."

Easing into his chair, Frost stabbed a piece of chicken and plunked it on Charles' plate. "Sit back down, my friend, and enjoy the rest of your meal." When Charles sat beside him, he added, "You've helped me before. Now I need more help. That's the way you can repay me."

George rolled his eyes but didn't respond.

When Mrs. George entered bearing a freshly baked blackberry pie, she frowned at her husband. "What was all that yelling about, William? I could hear you from the other room."

Charles spoke up. "Oh, it's nothing, Mrs. George. It's all settled now."

She looked at the bills still in her husband's hand. "I see. We'll discuss this later, George." She reached for the money and slipped it into her apron pocket. "Now, let's finish our meal on a pleasant note."

Turning to Nathaniel, she fired questions at him. "And how are you feeling, Mr. Frost? Didn't you go to the doctor today? What kind of report did he give you? Any new medicine?"

A coughing spell that wouldn't stop relieved him of the obligation to respond, as he had to leave the table. Mrs. George followed with a glass of water, which he waved off, stammering out, "I need to go to my room, get cough syrup."

She didn't follow, but Charles did. Taking Nathaniel's arm, he steadied him down the hall to the bedroom, pulled down the covers, removed his shoes, and helped him into bed.

Nathaniel coughed out a, "Thank you," as he remained in a sitting position. "I, uh, I, uh, need some medicine." He coughed harder.

Charles looked around. "I don't see any medicine bottles. Where is it?"

Squinting, Nathaniel replied, “In my, uh, wait. Get me the basin.”

Charles handed it to him, and Frost spit bloody phlegm into it, coughing so heavily his whole body shook. “Are you all right, Nate?” *Oh,God! This looks awful. He’s not going to die on me, is he?*

A bang on the door announced Mrs. George’s voice. “Are you all right, Mr. Frost? Can I do anything for you?”

Nathaniel shook his head and waved his hands, saying, “Don’t let her in. Tell her I’m better.”

Charles honored his wishes, and Mrs. George replied. “Well, please let me know if I can help.”

Between coughs, Nathaniel managed to speak. “The medicine is laudanum, so I only take it when I must. I hid it in my secret place.” He narrowed his eyes. “I, uh, I have some money in there, too.” He grabbed Charles’ wrist and stared into his eyes. “I’ll trust you. But never tell another soul.”

Charles swallowed hard. Nodding, he followed his friend’s finger pointing to the rug between their beds. He knelt on the floor, lifted the carpet, and stared back at his friend while forcing his eyes wide open.

“Surprised? Then I’ve kept my secret well, haven’t I?”

“You have indeed,” Charles lied. Before waiting for further instructions, he pulled the hinged lid open, took out the box, and exclaimed, “Aha, so what’s in this box, Nate?” He focused on the object. “It’s locked.”

Nathaniel dug a key out of the back of a drawer full of his clothes. “Give me the box.” He reached out his hands.

Hanging onto the object, Charles said, “You’re still shaky, why don’t you let me get out what you want? Give me the key.”

“No, I can do it myself.” He kept his hand clenched on the key and suppressed a cough.

Charles nodded, but didn’t release the box. *If he takes out money, he’ll know some is missing. He’ll see the IOU’s I left there, but that won’t appease him, at least not much. He’ll know he can’t trust me. I can’t let that happen. What am I going to do? How can I stop him from discovering...”*

While rising, Charles pretended to trip on the rug. With a little push of his foot, the box slid across the room and under his own bed. When Nathaniel got out of bed to help retrieve it, Charles bumped into him, and he grabbed Charles’ arm, dropping the key in the process.

“Sorry,” Charles told his friend. “I’ll get the box.” He glanced around the floor for the key but didn’t spot it. He helped Nate back in bed, pulled the box out, and left it by the rug. Then he scrambled around and found the key next to the lid. Without permission, he unlocked the box.

Before he could check for the IOU’s, Nate reached over and snatched the box out of his hands. Money and slips of paper fell all over the bed covers, and Nate scrambled to gather them up. He squinted at one piece of paper. “What’s this say? I can barely read it. Looks like your signature, Charles. What! It’s an IOU!” He dropped it and glared at his friend. “Omigod! You’ve found my box and taken my money. How could you, Charles?” He shook a fist. “I thought you were my friend. I trusted you.” His voice trembled.

Charles sat on the bed beside him. “I am your friend. I needed money so badly. My creditors have repeatedly applied to me for payment. I came across your box by accident when the rug slid aside one day." He put his arm around his friend's shaky shoulders. "I've helped you, and I know you appreciate that. I wasn't stealing from you; I only borrowed the money. The IOU's prove my intention to pay you back." He tightened his grip on Nathaniel's shoulders. "You don't really mind, do you?"

Wheezing, Nathaniel cocked his head. "How much did you take?" Before Charles could respond, he added, "I saved that money to buy eyeglasses and for my consumption medicine. It's getting worse. I haven't told you, but I need to go to the hospital and that's very expensive." He sighed. "My bosses don't know this either, but I don't think I'll be able to work much longer." He looked up at Charles. "But I need to keep working. There's not much left for me to live on, even less than I thought since you took my money. What am I going to do?"

"I'll help you, just like I always do." He placed his hand on Nathaniel's arm. "You know I've always taken care of you even though your disease, uh, well, consumption is responsible for one out of every four deaths. No matter, we'll manage," his words seemed to restore some of Nathaniel's trust.

As Charles returned the contents to the box and put it back in its cubbyhole, he slipped some of the money into his pocket. *Maybe things weren't too bad after all.* Nathaniel's inability to stay on the job gave him a plan. Next week, he'd implement it.

#

Charles headed for Pollard and Dale the following Friday when he knew his roommate would be out for lunch. Nate always went to Bienville Square to sit on the park bench and eat the peanut butter and jelly sandwich Mrs. George fixed for him. She also added carrot sticks, a piece of cake, and a jar of freshly squeezed orange juice.

Charles had met his friend at the park a couple of times, so he knew the routine. Nate would feed crumbs of bread to the squirrels and chat with elderly gentlemen lounging around. Veterans frequented the park, some from the War of 1812 and two or three from the Revolutionary War. Nate would be gone for his full lunch hour.

Walking into the print shop office, Charles' former boss greeted him without rising from his desk. "How are you Charles? What can I do for you today?"

"I'm fine, Mr. Pollard. But I still need work. I hope business has picked up and you can give me back my old job."

Pollard stood and shook his head. "Sorry, Charles. Nothing has changed. Business is still very slow." He brushed past his former employee. "Excuse me. I have to get this copy to the back. Frost will need it as soon as he returns from lunch."

Gritting his teeth, Charles followed Pollard into the back of the shop, keeping pace with his steps. "Mr. Pollard," he said, "Do you know how ill Frost is? He told me he won't be able to work much longer."

"Balderdash! That's hogwash. Why the man is always on time and he works late."

"But, Sir, his consumption is worse. He had a spell yesterday and he told me he needs to go to the hospital. He's surviving on medication. He also has ocular tuberculosis and his eyesight's failing. Sooner or later he'll start making costly mistakes." He tugged on his former boss's sleeve. "Hire me back, and I'll prove to you I can do the job better than he's been doing. I'm a damn good printer. You know that."

Pollard pulled free. "Let me go. Mr. Boyington, you never did your job as you should have. I don't believe Frost is that bad off.

Besides, I wouldn't hire you back if he was." He took long strides as he hurried away.

Charles stormed out and headed back to the boarding house so he would be on time for dinner. Otherwise, he'd have to miss a meal. He'd save the money he'd pilfered for gambling.

At the table, George asked Charles, "Have you secured employment yet?"

Clearing his throat after swallowing food, Charles replied, "I've just left my former employ ers, and I think they'll have something soon, maybe part-time." Charles rubbed his chin. *Better to say part-time—I don't want them to raise my rent.*

"I see." George squinted at Charles. "You'll have another month's rent due soon—very soon—next Friday, in fact." He leaned forward in his chair. "I don't think Frost will take care of it again. Will you be able to pay it on time, Charles?"

"Yes, I will. I have some friends I'm asking for assistance." He bit into a biscuit, savoring its melting in his mouth, his mind clicking. He'd called on some friends up north again, expecting a reply by May first. But that date had come and gone, and he'd received no reply.[2]

"You've been late often," George reminded him. "We need to pay bills, too, I have another party interested in renting your room. And Nathaniel is agreeable to share with him."

Charles shoved back his chair and stood. "Mr. George, I actually paid in advance once. I will have the money on time. I've written several poems that I think I can sell to Pollard and Dale." *That statement isn't entirely false. I have written lots of poems. But can I sell them?* He left the dining room, went to his bedroom, pulled a tablet out of a drawer, and reread one of his poems:

No. II.

THE WANDERER

Air—"The Minstrel's Return."

A youth, who had long from his hoe,

And all that he loved been afar,

While doom'd unbefriended to roam,

Thus sang to his tuneful guitar:--

"The joys of youth now no more

Inspiringly ring on my ear;

The transports I've felt oft before,

Now nought but a vision appear;

The prospects and pleasures of youth

Will vanish, alas, ere the morrow,

And, unveiling, reveal the sad truth

That this life's but a valley of sorrow."

He paused—a tear sat in his eye,

But he conquered his feelings again,

And while he suppressed a deep sigh,

He continued his mournful strain"

"The hopes that I once fondly cherished,

Have vanished ere scarce they began,--

Like the dew 'fore the sun, they have perish'd,

When the landscape of morning we scan.

The prospects and pleasures of youth &c.

"My eye hath lost nought of its fire,

This brow is unwrinkled with care,

Yet my dearest hopes did expire,

And vanish, like mist, into air.

I've sail'd o'er the tempestuous ocean,

Where dark lower'd the threatening sky,

And while I gazed on its commotion,

In sorrowful accents I'd cry—

The prospects and pleasures of youth," &c.

Mobile, March, 1834 AEOLIAN.[3]

Tears filled his eyes. *Ah, I am a wanderer. Those words express my feeling so clearly. I wish I had a mandolin so I could put them to music.*

He glanced at another poem he intended to include in his Young Rambler's Port Folio, made minor corrections, and then put it aside. Then he went to meet Rose at a predetermined spot. He needed to see her to lift his spirits.

Lydia was on Broad Street when he arrived. She motioned him to follow her, and they went into the wooded area where Rose sat on a blanket next to azalea bushes.

Charles pulled his sweetheart to a standing position and kissed her on first one cheek and then the other. Then he backed away, holding her at arms' length.

"Rosa, my dear, it seems so long since I've seen you."

Her eyes twinkled. "It's only been a week."

"Oh, but that's an eternity to me," Charles took a sheet of paper from his pocket and read a poem to her:

TO A BUTTERFLY AT CHRISTMAS

Oh care-free creature,

Flitting here and flitting there;

You should be tucked in

From this chilly air.

You press each flower

With a kiss and a smile;

I wish I were a butterfly

For just a little while.

Oh to be a care-free creature,

You never fret or cry,

Whose happiness is only

Flowers and rainless sky!

Then take me with you

To Titania's flow'ry home

There to rest in peace,

Never more to roam.[4]

"That expresses how I feel, my dearest, and I'm going to have it published to prove my love for you to all the world." He kissed her on the lips, and she didn't resist.

"My wonderful Robert," she said, "how I've missed you, too." Tears formed in her eyes. "I must tell you my father is insisting that I do not see you anymore. I don't know what to do. He's threatened to ban me from his home. Where would I go?"

"What does your mother say?"

"She defends me, but you know how it is. Father doesn't listen to her. Women don't have any rights."

He took her hand in his. "Will you go away with me?"

Rose's eyes widened. "Where could we go? How could we survive? You don't have a job, and I don't have any money of my own."

"Love conquers all." Charles pulled Rose close and kissed the tip of her nose. "I'd find a way. I do have a trade, Rosa, my dear. Printers are in demand other places. We could go to New Orleans. I bet I could get a job there."

Rose backed away. "My dear Charles, it's too risky for both of us. I'd love to go with you; you know that. Maybe you could go ahead, get a job, and then send for me."

Charles' brow wrinkled. "Is that our only choice? How can I live without you, even for a while?"

Lydia came over and placed her hand on Rose's arm. "We must be going, Rose, or your father will send someone looking for us."

She turned to Charles, "I'm sorry to make you part."

"I understand."

Charles turned to Rose with a kiss and a promise. "I'll figure out how we can be together. Meet me here tomorrow at noon. I'll find a way."

They separated. Charles went toward the Roper house under construction. Maybe he could get a job helping build it. Even though he had no skills working with his hands, they could teach him. But he didn't get the chance to apply. No workmen were there. Progress seemed slow. Some walls were up, but the floor plan wasn't easily discerned. Still, it was obvious that this structure would have many rooms.

If I had a house a fourth this size and a job, Rose and I could live comfortably. Why do some people have all the money, all the luck? As it is, I can't even provide her a simple living arrangement, which is in direct opposition to the lifestyle to which she's accustomed. And her lifestyle is one I'd like to become accustomed to!

He picked up a twig and snapped it in half. *But I'll be damned if that, or anything else, is going to stop me. Come hell or high water, Rose and I are going to be together.*

He left the woods, crossed Broad Street, and passed some time making his way through the Church Street Graveyard. No need to hurry. The poker game wouldn't start for a couple of hours. Since gambling was his only recourse, the backroom was his destination. He repeated positive thoughts of good results aloud. "I vow I'm going to win tonight, some way, somehow." He'd never cheated at cards before, but he felt he could do so without getting caught. And his situation made him frantic enough to take that chance if necessary.

TWELVE
A LITTLE LUCK

With cash in his hand, Charles walked into Stony's back room and handed a few bills to Tommy John. "Here's a payment on my account." He pulled out a chair and sat in it. A waitress entered with a tray of beers, and Charles took one. "I'll win tonight and pay you a little more." He swigged down some beer.

"Ya betta hurry. I got a cold, so I ain't staying too long. What do ya say, fellows," Frog blurted out in a hoarse voice, "do we limit this here young'un to three hands unless he's winnin'?"

The other men at the table nodded.

Charles took out a handkerchief and coughed into it. "Playing a few hands suits me. I've got a cold, too." *I'll leave when I'm winning.*

The first two hands, Charles lost, but not much. The third one, he dealt, and he managed to slip two aces from the bottom of the deck. He bet heavily and came out a winner. He faked a coughing spell, gulped down the rest of his glass of beer, and said, "I've got to leave." He coughed again. "This cold's getting to me."

Gathering his winnings, he tossed a five-dollar-bill to Tommy John. "Here's another payment." He shook a finger in his direction. "I told you I was good for it."

"Yeah," Tommy John replied. "But that's a piddling amount considering what you owe. You better come up with the rest, and soon, Charles." "Don't worry; I will." Charles let the door slam behind him as he left.

Out on the street, he jumped into the air and let his heels click. He fingered the paper money and the coins in his pocket. He chuckled at having told Tommy John not to worry when, *he* was the one who didn't have to worry. Everything looked good. In less than fourteen hours, he'd be with his love making plans for the future, and what grand plans they were.

By 11:45 a.m. the next day, Charles awaited Rose by the tree near the Roper house. The workmen pounding away with hammers didn't see him, but he watched them

from his vantage point. Birds chirped, and squirrels ran rampant in the area. Charles whistled a tune as he kept an eye out for Rose.

When he heard a rustling in the bushes, he rushed in the sound's direction and found Rose. "I slipped away without Lydia," she said. "I don't want to get her in trouble, but I want to be alone with you." She fell into Charles' arms, and he held her tight, kissing her over and over.

"Rose, oh, Rosa, my dear. I love you so much. I am world-weary, but you are the light of my life, my shining star. You are more beautiful than any flower." He took a step back, reached into his pocket, and held coins and folding money in the palm of his hand. "I have some money, and I have a plan. We can go away together and get married. Get a new start." He leaned over and kissed her forehead. "Say you are willing."

"Oh, Charles, I shouldn't. I really shouldn't. But…"

He pulled her close. "But you should. Two people in love need to be together no matter the cost. Trust me. I will take care of you. Please, my love, please agree to go with me."

She snuggled her head against his chest. "My head says 'No' but my heart says 'Yes.'"

Charles exhaled. "Here's the plan. I have some business with my melancholy friend Nathaniel, and I must say goodbye to him. But he's the only one I'll tell I'm leaving. To keep it private, we'll take a walk after dinner, and I'll meet you here at five o'clock. We can…"

A scream interrupted. "Rose, Rose, where are you? Your father's…"

Without further ado, Rose pecked Charles on the cheek, and then ran toward the sound of Lydia's voice. "Tomorrow, my dearest, tomorrow," she called over her shoulder as she blew multiple kisses to him.

Charles sauntered out of the wooded area, whistling again. The interruption didn't matter. He had no intention of telling Rose all of his plans.

THIRTEEN

THE LAST DAY

The smell of roast beef wafted from the dining room to Charles' bedroom, increasing his hunger. He headed for the dining room.

Nathaniel's consumption had become worse, so he had to retire at the end of April. He now spent most of his time at the boarding house. Coughing almost incessantly, on Saturday, May 10, 1834, he came to the table for dinner at half-past one p.m. with a handkerchief covering his mouth.[1]

Charles sat beside his friend, planning to eat a lot because he didn't know when he'd get his next full meal. He took large helpings of meat, potatoes, carrots, corn, and a biscuit. "Mmm, Mrs. George," he said, "you've outdone yourself. These biscuits are delicious. They melt in your mouth."

Mrs. George beamed. "Why thank you, Charles. I'm glad you're enjoying them. Save some room for pie."

Captain George curled his lip. "Saving isn't what Charles is best at," he sneered.

Charles fumbled around in his pocket. "Hmm, I saved money for my rent, but I must have left it in my room. I'll pay you later today."

"Humph! I won't hold my breath."

Charles shrugged.

After dinner, neither Nathaniel nor Boyington left the house until past three o'clock. Then the two men spent time on the piazza together. One boarder came out teasing Charles. "Ah, Frost tells me he showed you how to carve a heart for your girlfriend. You must be very sweet on her. I heard you were engaged. Is that right, Charles?"

Charles nodded, "Maybe it is." He didn't like the fellow, so he turned his back, and the man left. No one else was with them as he and Nate chatted about Mr. Williamson, and work at the printing shops being slow. Nate took out his carving knife saying, "You could use this time when you're not working to make another trinket for your girlfriend."

About half-past three, Frost left and went into the house, and Charles decided he would go to Spring Hill that evening. As he passed the door, Nate came out of the dining room.[2]

Charles helped his friend down the steps, asking, "Are you all right? Where are you going?"

"Just for a walk. Do you want to go with me?" He pulled out his carving knife.

We can go sit in the graveyard, and I'll show you how to carve something else for Rose."

"I have some business downtown first. If you feel like going that way, we'll go together."

Mrs. Creighton, another boarder who was seated at the window on the south end of the house, stopped them and mentioned something to Frost about blackberries while Charles continued on his way. Before he reached Government Street, Nathaniel overtook him, and they discussed an herb Nathaniel was eating as recommended by his physician and of treatment his physician prescribed.

Charles said they parted along the way and he went down St. Emanuel Street and Church Street to Smith's stable on Royal Street, arriving before four p.m.[3] Out of hearing and out of sight.

#

Later that Saturday afternoon, Charles sneaked into his room, retrieved his belongings, and confiscated the rest of Nathaniel's money hidden under the rug. Then he bought two pistols, and a dirk knife, and went to Mr. Smith's livery stable. Since the horse Charles had previously engaged had *gone to the races*, he took a white horse to go on Spring Hill road. After riding it a short distance, he decided it trotted too rough. He returned the horse and went back to Captain George's boarding house.[4]

With shaky hands, Charles handed his landlord a packet. "This is for Rose; please see that she gets it." He recalled the words he'd written in his last note to her:

Rosa, My Dear,

I will not meet you this evening, for I must go away for a while until I feel better. I have left a package containing my books, my letters, and the miniature of my mother, and I have written a note instructing Mrs. George, the landlady to give them to you. Keep them and remember me always, Rose, my dear.

Mobile, May 10, 1834
ROBERT."[5]

"Are you going somewhere? What about my rent?" His landlord interrupted his thoughts.

"No," Charles lied. "I'll be back later tonight." Without further explanation, and before George could question him further, he darted out of the house. Almost on a run, he headed for the wharf where the steamboat James Monroe would leave between eight and nine o'clock that evening. He had a boat to catch and he didn't intend to miss it.[6]

FOURTEEN

THE MURDER

Early Sunday morning, May 11, 1834, a group of Mobilians strolling through the pinewoods near the pathway behind the old cemetery spotted something that stopped them—a body spread eagle facing the ground. What they'd discovered was a man stabbed to death, lying in a clump of gallberry bushes.[1]

"Oh, dear God!" a woman gasped as she made the Sign of the Cross.

One of the men accompanying her stooped to see several blood spots from wounds and bruises on the body's head. The absence of any sign of a pulse made it clear that the victim was dead. He got to his feet and called, "Help!" No response. He turned to a teenager in the group. "Go get the sheriff. Hurry."

The boy took off in a run to the sheriff's office to report the crime.

Before he'd run one block, a horse trotted toward him. "Stop!" the young man yelled. He pointed to the cemetery gate. "There's a dead body over there."

Sheriff Joseph Bates, Jr. said, "Follow me," and headed in that direction. When he reached the scene, he got off his horse and stared at the corpse. Turning it over, he shook his head. "Hell, it's Nathaniel Frost, that printer at Pollard and Dale." He turned to the group of four. "What do you folks know about this?"

One man spoke up, shaking his head. "We were just out for a walk and happened to come across this unfortunate man."

"Oh, I wish I'd never seen it," the woman said as she turned her face away from the dead body.

"I, uh, I don't know nothin', I swear. I, uh…" the boy stammered, waving around trembling hands.

"Okay, Son." Bates looked at the members of the group up and down. "You ain't got no blood on you." He scratched his chin. "I've seen you people around. Give me your names and addresses." He handed a pad and pencil over.

One man gave the sheriff the information, and then the sheriff told the group, "I'll stay here and investigate. You know where my office is?"

The boy nodded. "Yes, sir, I do. I was headed there…"

"Okay. One of you men escort these ladies home." He pointed to the young man. "You go tell my deputy to come here pronto, with the coroner. You understand?"

Nodding, the young man replied. "I'll do it," and took off in a run.

He looked at the other man. "You follow the boy. Be careful, a murderer may be loose around here."

Members of the group headed in different directions.

Taking out a notepad and a pencil, the sheriff wrote: "May 11, 1834--Body – Nathaniel Frost—His friend—Boyington reported missing 9 a.m. by Mrs. George."[3] Then he stooped to study the wounds, jotting down, "6 stab wounds – weapon, a dirk,

bruises to the head, watch cut from its fob." Frost's carving knife was not found at the scene. The body was on top of the tomb of Asceneth Alexander Korbets, wife of Dr. Willis Roberts, City physician who died on 3 Feb. 1833.[2]

Bates lifted the man's frail arm and let it drop. Standing, he pulled on his Adam's apple. "Damn it to hell, this fellow wasn't strong enough to defend himself. He didn't have a chance."

#

The late afternoon of the day before the murder, Patsey, a milkmaid for the Lawson family, watched the family's milk cow graze in a grassy area behind the Church Street Cemetery. After it finished, she tied a rope around its neck and walked toward the Lawson's shed.

As she passed the edge of the Old Church Street Cemetery wall, Patsey heard shouting and cursing, one voice deeper, louder and angrier than the other.[4]

"Where's the money?" demanded the person with the deeper voice.

"You've taken all I have," the weaker voice said. "Let me go."

"We know you have more hidden somewhere. Where is it?" the angrier voice said.

"You're mistaken," said the insistent respondent.

"Oh, Lawdy, lemme git away from here." Patsey tightened her grip on the rope.

She walked ahead of the cow and pulled on its rope to hurry her across the street, away from the cemetery, and out of sight of the shouting people. In spite of her urging and strongest pull, the cow kept her slow pace.

The sun dropped lower in the sky and cast an orange-yellowish glow on the shiny clusters of pine needles on the branches of the tall, narrow pine trees. Layers of fallen pine straw muffled the sound of Patsey's hasty footsteps.

The cow ambled along with its feet sinking deeper into the cushion of pine straw, slowing their pace.

When Patsey had walked about forty yards, she passed well-groomed front yards and large houses with wide porches. As she guided the cow off the pine straw and onto the street, the lumbering animal's feet click-clacked on the brick road.

Now that she was safely away from the cemetery and near houses, Patsey stopped and turned to look toward the graveyard.

The two people were still fighting in the deep shadows of the trees. One deep male voice could still be heard, but it no longer echoed down the narrow street.

The figure of the shorter one caught her attention as the person barreled toward the taller one. The tall one raised his arms in front of their chest, but the shorter one immediately grabbed the other person's wrists with a single twisting motion and then shoved the opponent down on the ground with a thud.

No longer in the shadows, wide beams of sunshine shone on the two and the patch of land on which the taller of the two had fallen.

Patsey saw the shorter person walk to the old wall slam an object against the head of the fallen victim.

After a minute or so passed, she saw a single glint of light reflect off a long object held up in the air by the oppressor who bent down and brought the shiny, long object to the fallen man's chest.

Patsey squinted as she focused on counting the number of times the victim was struck. On the sixth motion of what looked like a long knife blade going into the now motionless man's chest, she turned toward the opposite end of the street.

The rope fell from Patsey's hand as she heard a harrowing scream, one she had never heard before. She lifted her hands to cover her mouth. The street became totally silent.

Patsey picked the rope up off the ground, and her steps quickened. She walked another block before she saw any people. As she got closer to a house in the center of a side street, she saw the Lawson's teenaged neighbors, Ralph and James, sitting on the bottom step of James' front porch. James was bouncing a small red rubber ball.

"I'm glad to see you, Master James and Master Ralph," Patsey said in a high-pitched, breathless voice. "They's trouble down by that old cemetery wall. Two people, men I think, are shoutin' and fightin' there. Oh, lawsy, one of 'em let out a horrible scream."

"I told you I heard a scream," James said to Ralph. "I thought it was a stray cat."

"You think we should go take a look?" Ralph said.

"No, sirs, you young men don't be walkin' down there to that old wall. Somethin' bad and fearsome is happenin' there." Patsey threw up her hands and shook them. "I'm goin' to the Lawsons' house to put the cow in the shed. Then I'm ah-goin' tah run tah whar I stay and lock the doah, sure as I'm standin' right here." Patsey quickened her pace down the road with the cow in tow.[5]

The two wide-eyed teenagers stood.

"Let's go check the graveyard, then I'll go tell my father." James slipped the ball into his shirt pocket.

"I'm not telling mine," Ralph said. "Patsey was afraid. Did you see her hand shaking as she held that rope?" Ralph held out his right hand and shook it like a quivering reed.

“I am not going to tell my parents what Patsey said. What if those men are robbers and come looking for us? I’m going home and not coming back out tonight,” Ralph said.

“Then there’s no sense in me walking down to that old graveyard alone.” James wiped his forehead with his sleeve. His voice had a note of relief. James was two years older than Ralph, so it made sense he had the final say on the matter.

“I’ll see you tomorrow.” Ralph walked away. “Please don’t tell your father I was here. I’m supposed to be working in the yard clearing out pine straw for my mother’s garden.”

“I won’t. Don’t worry. My father will know what to do.” James climbed five steps and turned the handle on his solid wood front door.

Ralph ran down the center of the street in the same direction Patsey had walked moments earlier, ignoring the sound of crickets and the sight of the late afternoon sun as it dipped beneath the tops of the trees in the piney woods near the cemetery.

Unsure that his father would acknowledge that a slave’s story had any credibility, James hesitated to make a decision. Before he reached home, he’d convinced himself that he didn’t see anything; he didn’t know anything. The scream he’d heard could’ve been a cat. Patsey could’ve made up her story to get attention. Nope, Ralph was right. “Don’t say nothin’.” What came next changed his mind, but his own credibility became questionable.

#

Even before Nathaniel Frost’s murder made the newspaper headlines, many of Mobile’s 3,190 residents got wind of it, in bars, pool halls, and in churches during Sunday services. They flocked to the scene to get a look at the spot where it occurred. Speculation ran rampant. Some said of the deceased, “Oh, he was a fine, hardworking man." Others degraded Frost as being "a slacker who pretends to be ill."

They came up with many theories as to the murderer's identity, running the gamut from Boyington to Captain George. Some accused a woman nobody seemed to know.

James couldn't hold back. He blurted out to his father what Patsey told him.

"Humph! Don't even bother to call her in here. I don't believe a word of it. Patsey's just trying to act important. If you even thought it was true, why didn't you check on it?"

"But, Father, she told Ralph and me this yesterday afternoon. Sheriff Bates didn't know about the murder till this morning. How could…"

"Boy, can't you figure anything out? Maybe she heard a ruckus down by the graveyard, but fights go on there all the time. Probably a couple of drunks. Just a coincidence a murder happened there. Could've been today, the next day. Besides all that, even if Patsey did see or hear something, it wouldn't matter. Slaves can't testify in court. Forget it." He walked away, leaving his son befuddled.

First Jail in Mobile
Remodeled in 1850
(Conde-Charlotte House)

Historic Marker
Charlotte House Jail

Broken glass bottles embedded in wall of Conde' - Charlotte House

Mobile Riverfront

Oakleigh House Museum

Church Street Graveyard

Church Street Graveyard

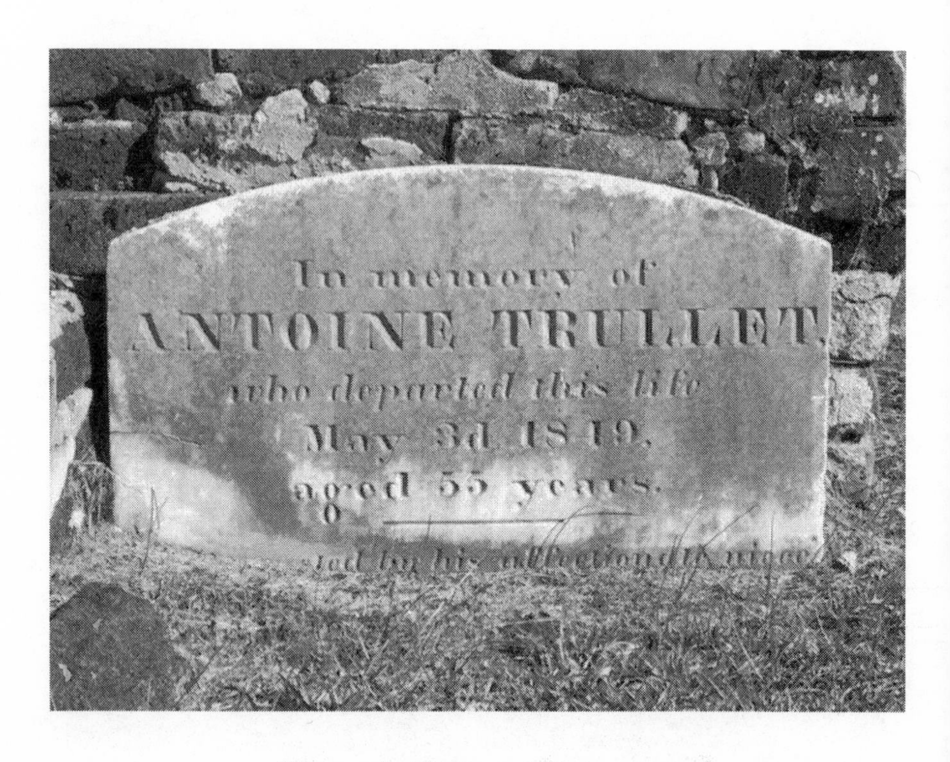

Church Street Graveyard

Church Street Graveyard

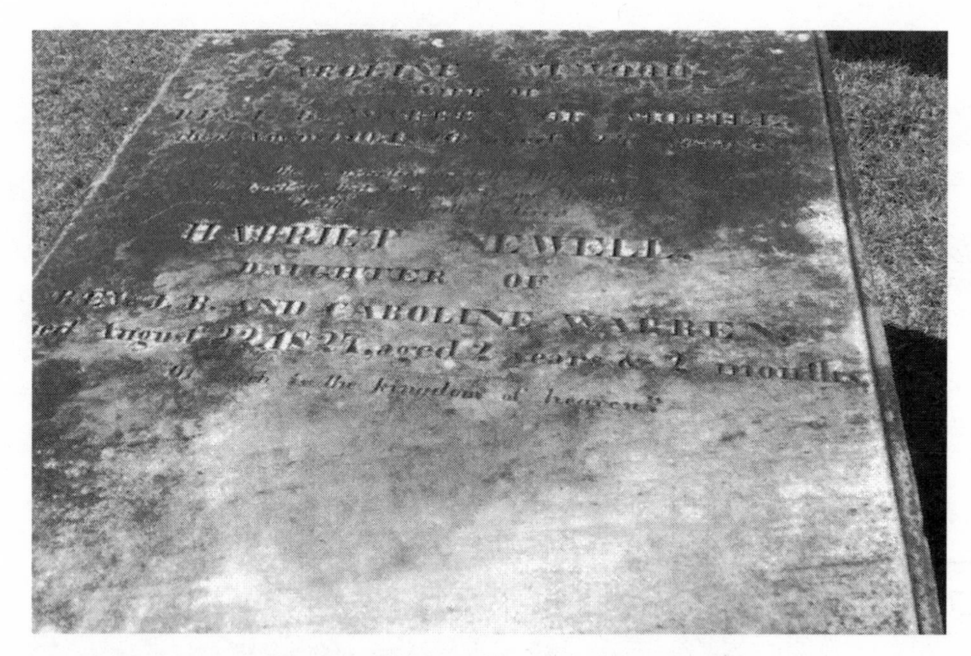

Church Street Graveyard

Church Street Graveyard

Church Street Graveyard

Church Street Graveyard

Shannon Brown and Mary S. Palmer

Visitation Convent Chapel

Mary S. Palmer, Preston Boyington, Shannon Brown.

Mobile Merchantile Advertiser
Volume 1 Number 180
17 May 1834 Saturday Morning
Page 2 Column 1

Magistrates Court- Thour set on yesterday for the trial of Boyington, arrested on suspicion of having murdered Nathaniel Frost, was ten o'clock, morning. From this time until near sunset the magistrates court was occupied in taking testimony in relation to the charges, and the result of the investigation was a commitment for trial at the next Circuit Court. In the justice of this decision we do most cordially acquirdvr, at the same time we cannot refrain from wondering, that not one syllable was uttered on this occasion, about admitting this unfortunate young man to bail- more especially as such a course is not without a precedent in this city.

Mobile Commercial Register And Patriot
22 November 1834
Saturday Evening
Page 2 Column 1

The trial of Charles Boyington for the murder of Nathaniel Frost, a crime which caused so great an excitement in this community at the time, came on Thursday. A jury was empannelled on that day, and the examination of the testimony was commenced yesterday moring, and occupied the whole of the day. The Counsel for the Prisoner summed up in his defence in the evening, and the case was closed for the prosecution, about 12 o'clock at night. The charge of the Judge was finished a little before 12 o'clock, and the Jury, after retiring for the space of an hour and a quarter, returned a verdict of Guilty.

The counsel for the prosecution were Solictor Breedin, and James Dillet, Esq. and for the Prisoner, Isaac H. Erwin, and Edward R. Olcott, Esquires.

The Court House was crowded during the whole trial, and up to the hour of the rendering of the verdict-and throughout the city it was the universal topic of conversation. Rarely have the feelings of the community been more deeply interested.- The murder was so cold blooded, so unprovoked, and so audacious, and the accused, so self possessed, during the whole of the bloody affair, from the crime to the conviction, that wonder, and horror, were mingled with the ordinary feelings of curiosity and excitement on such occasions.

Copious notes of the testimony were taken, which will be published as soon as they can be prepared.

Boyington Trial

Check list of Alabama imprints, 1807–1840
(American imprints inventory no. 8)
C16.9761 A

Boyington, Charles R. S., defendant
A Statement | of the | Trial of Charles R. S. Boyington, | who was indicted and executed | for the | Murder of Nathaniel Frost, | [short rule] Written by himself. [short rule] | To which is added, | a number of fugitive pieces in verse, | also written and composed by him. | [short double rule] | Mobile: | Printed at the office of the Mercantile Advertiser | [dash] | [1835] |
40 p. 13 X 21 cm

Henry E. Huntington Library, San Marino Cal. [2 copies]
Yale University Libraries, New Haven, Conn. [2]
~~Interstate Commerce Commission Library, Washington~~ [1]
Library of Congress, Washington, D.C. [33]
Charleston Library Society, Charleston, S.C. [1]

Trial Report

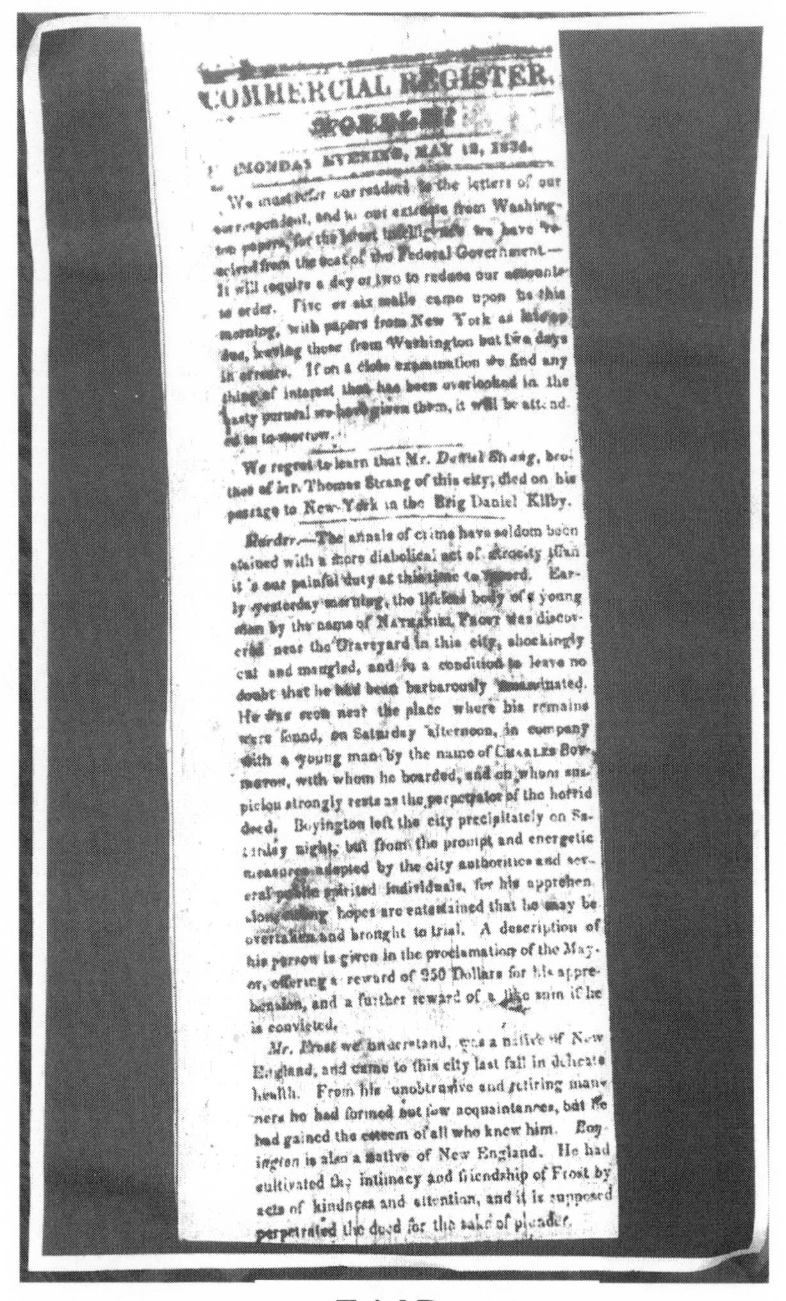

COMMERCIAL REGISTER.

[illegible]

MONDAY EVENING, MAY 18, 1834.

We must refer our readers to the letters of our correspondent, and to our extracts from Washington papers, for the latest intelligence we have received from the seat of the Federal Government.— It will require a day or two to reduce our accounts to order. Five or six mails came upon us this morning, with papers from New York as late as due, leaving those from Washington but two days in arrears. If on a close examination we find any thing of interest that has been overlooked in the hasty perusal we have given them, it will be attended to to-morrow.

We regret to learn that Mr. *Daniel Strang*, brother of Mr. Thomas Strang of this city, died on his passage to New-York in the Brig Daniel Kilby.

Murder.—The annals of crime have seldom been stained with a more diabolical act of atrocity than it is our painful duty at this time to record. Early yesterday morning, the lifeless body of a young man by the name of NATHANIEL FROST was discovered near the Graveyard in this city, shockingly cut and mangled, and in a condition to leave no doubt that he had been barbarously assassinated. He was seen near the place where his remains were found, on Saturday afternoon, in company with a young man by the name of CHARLES BOYINGTON, with whom he boarded, and on whom suspicion strongly rests as the perpetrator of the horrid deed. Boyington left the city precipitately on Saturday night; but from the prompt and energetic measures adopted by the city authorities and several public spirited individuals, for his apprehension, strong hopes are entertained that he may be overtaken and brought to trial. A description of his person is given in the proclamation of the Mayor, offering a reward of 250 Dollars for his apprehension, and a further reward of a like sum if he is convicted.

Mr. Frost we understand, was a native of New England, and came to this city last fall in delicate health. From his unobtrusive and retiring manners he had formed but few acquaintances, but he had gained the esteem of all who knew him. *Boyington* is also a native of New England. He had cultivated the intimacy and friendship of Frost by acts of kindness and attention, and it is supposed perpetrated the deed for the sake of plunder.

Trial Report

file 28 Pg. 2

County of Mobile
May 11th 1834 - To Jacob G. Collins Coroner Dr

	To inquisition in the Case of Nathaniel Forest	$10.00
	Summoning Jury of inquest	$2.00
		$12.00
May 18	To Summoning Jury and holding an inquest in the Case of a person unknown	12..00
June 13	To inquisition in the Case of Edward Murry and Summoning Jury inquest	12.25
June 14.	To inquisition in the Case of a person unknown and Summoning Jury of inquest	12.00
		$48.25

Received Mobile August 2nd 1834 from Jacob Collins Coroner of Mobile County, inquests in the above Cases making (four) —

J.G. Lyon clerk
Cir. Co. Mobile Cty.

Cost of Gallows

settled habits were often the despair of their employers, they were sometimes picturesque or even sensational characters, as in the case of the notorious Boyington, who was executed for murder in Mobile in 1835.[37] When Thomas Grantland, editor of the Tuscaloosa *Alabama Sentinel*, advertised for a journeyman printer in 1825, he was rewarded with an excellent publicity stunt. William Russell Smith records that an "eccentric and much traveled" printer named Singleton took the town by storm by offering a wager that he could set up the entire inside of the *Sentinel* (ten columns) in one day. "He did it," says Smith. "Crowds were collected about the doors and windows of the printing office looking at the lion of the hour.[38] During the forties and fifties the advertisements for printers continued, but not in such great number. At the end of the period office labor, like office supplies, became as scarce as at the beginning. The war took away printers and even apprentices. The *South Western Baptist* of February 25, 1864, quoted the *Macon Confederate* (edited by the former Mobilian, Henry Lynden Flash) as saying that during the war there were fewer papers printed in the whole Confederacy than before the war were published in Georgia alone, ascribing as the reason for the decline the fact that at least seventy-five per cent of the printers were in the army.

They themselves were a versatile lot—these editors who, in the face of all the difficulties of frontier conditions, undertook to bring the settlers their weekly ration of news, politics, and literature. Aside from their editorial function, they had

[37] William T. Hamilton, *The Last Hours of Charles R. S. Boyington Who Was Executed at Mobile, Alabama, for the Murder of Nathaniel Frost Perpretrated May 10, 1834* (Mobile: Printed at the Commercial Register Office, 1835).

[38] Smith, *op. cit.*, p. 21. Smith, who in his editorial days had been something of a practical printer himself, describes the old method of preparing the material for the hand press. After the types had been set by hand, the delicate job of removing them from the composing stick to the galley was accomplished by dipping a sponge in water and saturating the types. Then two semi-round balls, packed with wool and covered with leather, each having a handle in the center, were dabbed first in the ink box and then on the form as it lay on the press.

Execution Report

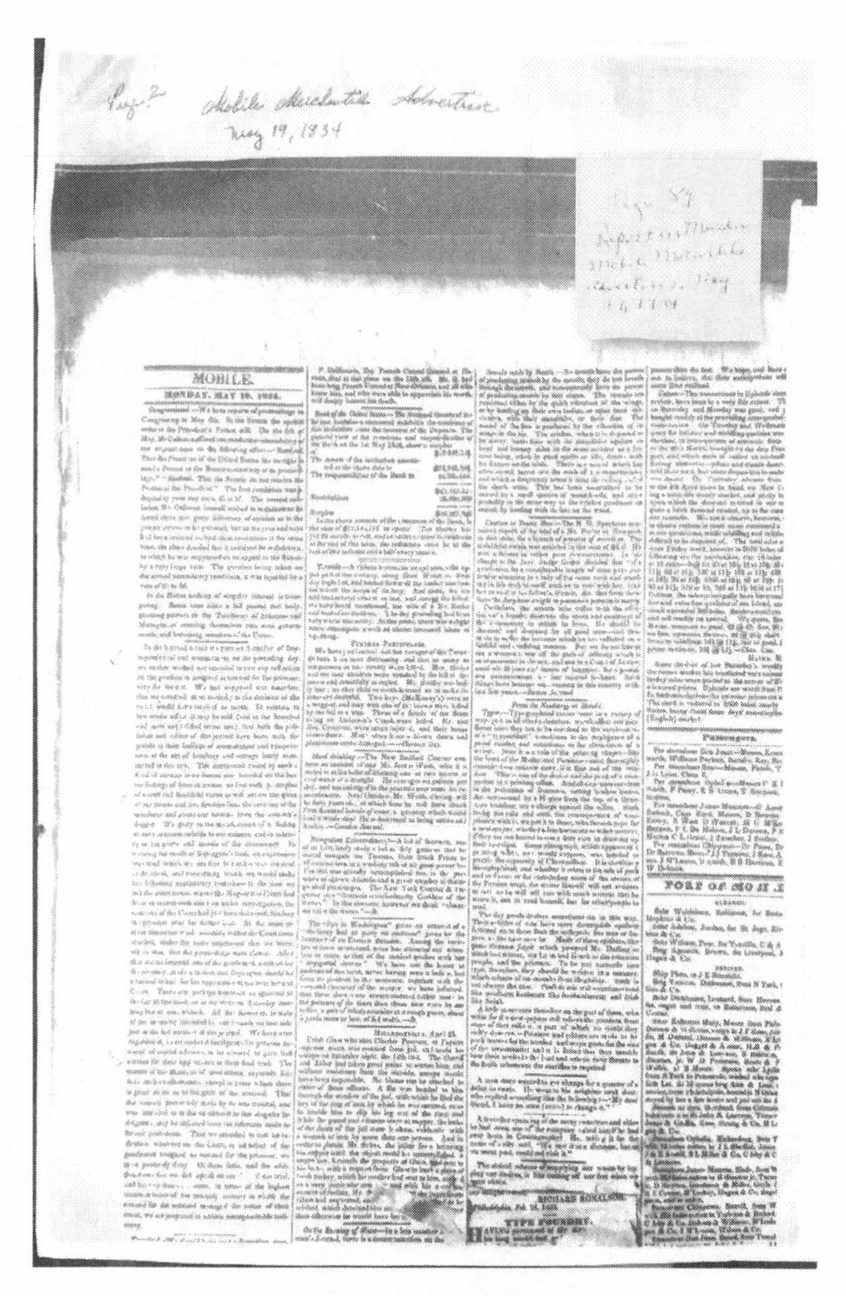

MOBILE.

MONDAY, MAY 19, 1834.

Report on Murder - Mobile Mercantile Advertiser, May 19, 1834

Nov. 3, 1834. Page 158.

Tuesday 4th November 1834. The Court met pursuant to adjournment present as before.

This morning after the Minutes of the Court of yesterday were read Isaac H. Erwin, Esq. an attorney of this Court suggested to the Court that one of the members of the Grand Jury Empannelled yesterday is not a citizen of the United States either by birth or naturalization - he also suggested that one other member of the said Grand Jury had expressed a sentiment very unfavorable to one Charles J. S. Boyington, the sentiment so expressed was that if he was on the jury to try him (said Boyington) he would hang him - said I. H. Erwin Esq. accompanied the above suggestion with a remark that he was present on yesterday when the Grand jury was empanelled and was apprised of the above facts but determined that he would not make the above suggestion at that time but at some subsequent period before any indictment found against Boyington.

Mobile Commercial Register And Patriot
16 May 1834
Friday Evening
Page 2 Column 1

Arrest of Boyington.- The steam boat Courier arrived last evening from Montgomery having on board Charles Boyington, the supposed murderer of Nathaniel Frost. We have never witnessed such an excitement as was manifested on his arrival. An immense throng rushed to the wharves and the anxiety was intense to obtain a sight of the man charged with having embued his hands in the blood of his friend. No disorder, however, occurred, and he wad conducted to the City Prison followed by the crowd, where he remains in irons under a strong guard during the night. At 10 o'clock this morning, he was taken to the Court House, where an examination was commenced and at the hour of sending our paper to press it had not been concluded.

Mobile Commercial Register And Patriot
15 May 1834
Thursday Evening
Page 2 Column 1

Arrest of Boyington.- We received positive intelligence this morning, that Boyington, the supposed murderer of Mr. Frost, has been taken.- A letter from the acting Post Master, at Claiborne, addressed to Col. H.H.R. Hays, states, that he was recognized among the passengers of the Steam Boat James Munroe, while she lay at the landing at that place, and that intelligence of the murder, with the circumstances attending it, reached there about three hours after the Boat had proceeded up the river. Mr. Joseph Taylor and Mr. M. Dubois, immediately stated on horseback, with the view to head the Boat at Black's Bluff, and happily succeeded in their object. They took passage for Canton, and on their way up secured the prisoner, and returned him to Claiborne. We regret to add that he succeeded in throwing overboard the watch, which was relied upon as furnishing the connecting link in the chain of circumstantial evidence to establish his guilt. He may be expected here in the course of two or three days.

Mobile Commercial Register And Patriot
21 February 1835
Saturday
Page 2 Column

Execution.-Yesterday at about 4 o'clock P.M. the extent of the time specified in the sentence, the execution of Boyington took place. He walked with a firm step from the prison to the gallows, a distance of two miles and a half, and having arrived there, mounted the scaffold, stood erect apparently unmoved, and delivered an address of nearly half an hour's length. To the last he made no acknowledgement of his guilt.- To say the least, however, it is a matter of doubt if his harrangue to the assembly did not excite prejudice against him, rather than sympathy in his behalf. The language he used was select and elegant, but it seemed rather argumentative than pathetic. On this count it was, perhaps, that it failed to awaken sympathy as might have been expected in such an emergency. The whole of his address, all of which was in manuscript, he was prevented from delivering, for want of time. Possibly the close might have exhibited touches of eloquence of a persuasive and feeling nature. We believe all will acknowledge he had the talent to shape an address in that manner if he chose to exert it. Whether it was so terminated, we have not understand. Almost the last words he uttered were that-'before God I am innocent of the crime for which I am about to die.

Mobile Commercial Register And Patriot
29 November 1834
Saturday Evening
Page 2 Column 2

After an arduous session of four weeks, the Circuit Court of this county adjourned about 4 P.M. A great deal of business had been dispatched, and a lean docket is left for the next term.

Prisoners convicted during the present term, were brought up this morning, and the sentences pronounced by Judge Chapman.

Charles Boyington for the murder of Nathaniel Frost-to be hanged on Friday, the 20th of February next-and

Wm. Allen for theft, to receive 39 lashes and be imprisoned until he restores the stolen property.

The delay in the case of Boyington is granted for the purpose of taking the opinion of the Supreme Court on some legal points raised by his consel. We shall endeavour to get for publication a copy of the Judge's charge, on pronouncing this judgement. It is represented to have been eloquent and impressive.

This is the first term in which Judge Chapman has presided. His ability and promptness in the discharge of business, has, we are gratified to learn, won for him the favorable regard of the bar, and the community.

MOSELY TUCKER.

Mobile, March 1, 1893.

For the Mercantile Advertiser: Copy of lines written in city prison Mobile, September, 1834—

THE PRISONER.

[Air—"All's well."]

From cell to cell echoes again
The clamoring of his pondrous chain;
The jailor opens his weary eyes,
And, starting from his couch, he cries
Hark!—whence that sound?—good night all's well.

Weary with care and long confined,
The prisoner sleeps, while thro' his mind
Flit scenes of pleasure that were past
Before he felt misfortune's blast:
He joyous shouts, but wakes at last
To hear—he's safe—good night—all's well.

Copy from "Young Rambler's Portafolio (Charles R. S. Boyington) written for the Mercantile Advertiser, Mobile, April, 1834.

MY MOTHER'S BLESSING—AT PARTING.

Her cheek was pale, her dark eyes sad,
As she breathed her last farewell;
And oft she sighed, yet blessed the while
Her tears in sorrow fell.
Her lip, that quivered as she spoke,
Was like the lily's hue,
And high her heart did beat, as low
She sighed a long adieu.

Warmly I pressed her trembling hands—
"Farewell, dear mother now;"
"God bless thee, boy,"—her heart was full—
They kissed my burning brow.
A tear fell on my warm flushed cheek,—
A mother's tear of love;—
"We soon must part," she said, "but we
Shall meet again above."

"When far hence, think oft, my son,
Of the days of youth and joy,
When all was happiness around,—
Forget not these, my boy,—
Remember then, how oft, in youth,
Thou'st rested on this breast,
And her who hath, in earlier days,
Thy infant form caress'd.

"Now go, be happy when afar,
But oh, do not forget
Thy mother, and thy mother's love—
A parent's deep regret.
May heaven 'round thy youthful brow
Entwine is brightest wreath,
And send its blessings bounteously
With this, my farewell breath."

AEOLIAN.

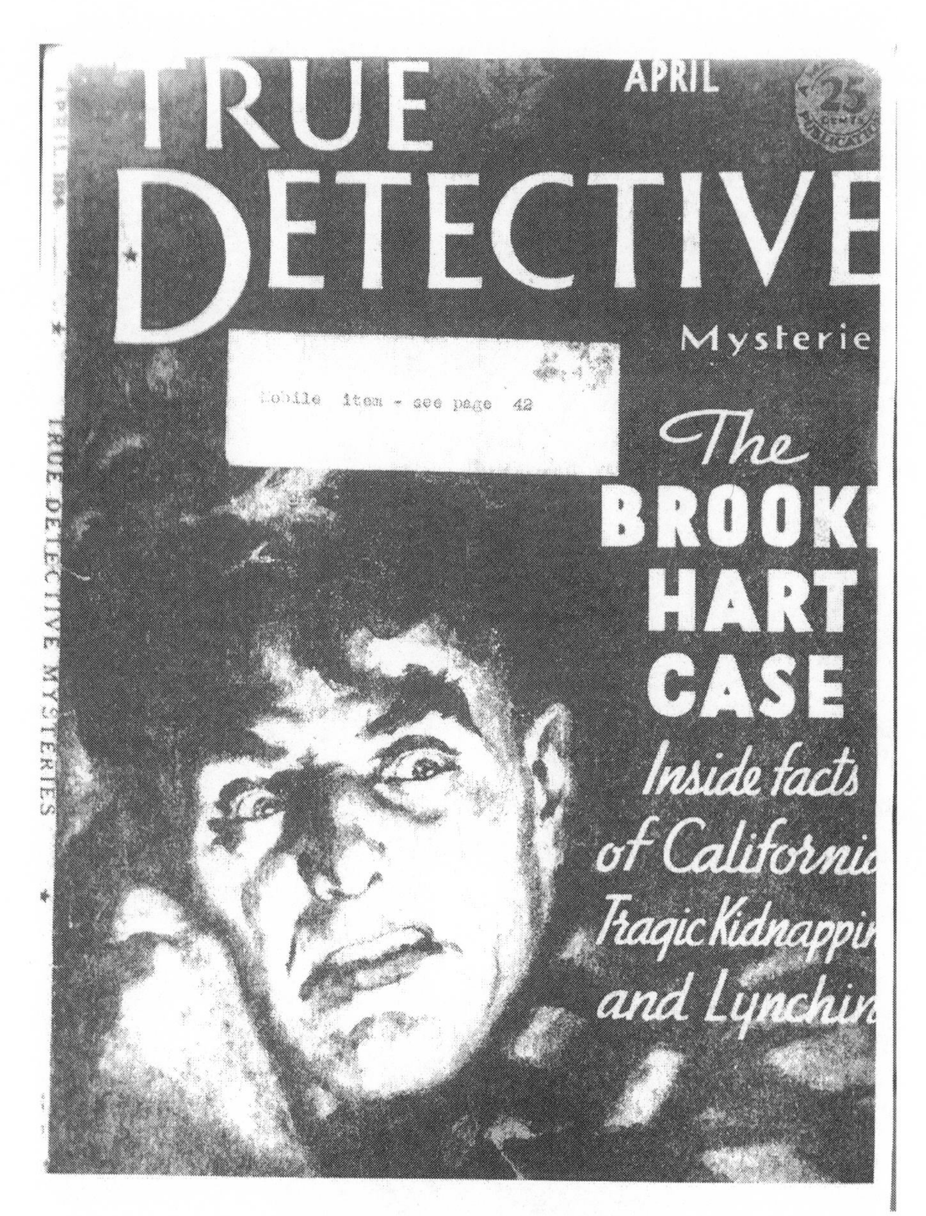

True Detective Magazine

lead for about fourteen or fifteen hours.

"What did you find on the body?" asked the solicitor.

"Only a little small change in one of his pockets. The fine gold watch and chain he always wore, his diamond ring and pocketbook that held his money were gone. Some of the pockets in his clothes were turned wrong side out."

"What motive can you ascribe for this murder?"

"Judging from all appearances, it was robbery."

After a short cross-examination by the defense counsel, this witness was dismissed. The two officers who arrested Boyington were called and their testimony showed that the cemetery-keeper had notified the police department as soon as the body was found. They then told how they had arrested Boyington; that they had searched him and found a wallet with money in it. This wallet had Frost's name on it.

"How much money was in the wallet?" This from Breeden.

"A little more than ninety-six dollars," was the answer.

"What else was in the wallet?"

"Some private letters addressed to Mr. Frost; some undue notes payable to Mr. Frost, and some IOU's signed by different people."

THE wallet was introduced in evidence and identified by the police officers.

"When you came upon the gangplank of the up-river steamer, did you see Mr. Boyington on the upper deck?"

"Yes, sir."

"What was he doing?"

"He was standing at the rail and threw overboard a large watch and chain that fell into the river near the gangplank where we were standing."

On cross-examination, Olcott asked: "How did you know it was a watch and chain?"

"I could see a large fob on the end of the chain and heard the clinking noise it made in falling."

"Can you swear positively that it was a watch and chain?"

"I am reasonably certain it was."

"Was any effort made to recover the watch?"

"Yes, sir. After the arrest, we dragged the river where it fell, but couldn't find it."

The attorney for the State rested the case.

The defense counsel placed on the stand many character witnesses who testified to the good moral character of Boyington. The latter then took the stand.

The prisoner told how he and Frost had been discussing a woman of the "Red Light District" when they entered the grounds, and then Boyington said:

"I was admonishing Frost, warning him to let her alone; that I was afraid she would bleed him for his money. We were not fighting, but our conversation at that point where the keeper overheard us, was more like good-natured banter."

The defense counsel then asked Boyington to tell the jury all that happened from the time he and Frost entered the cemetery until his arrest on the boat. To this request, he replied:

"We went into the cemetery to get away from the city for a walk. We sat down on a terrace near some thick evergreen shrubbery which was to our left side and against the wall. Frost and I talked about our stay in Mobile and other matters pertaining to what we were to do when we got back up the river. I was anxious for him to go with me, because I realized he'd been drinking entirely too much and I did not like the company he was running with while he was drinking. He, as well as myself, had won some money at cards during the last few days. When I could not persuade him to go with me, I gave him my bowie knife. Just before leaving him, he took the money from his wallet saying that when he had spent that, he would come home. He asked me to take it with the securities and IOU's, and keep it until he came."

The defense counsel then asked: "Did he also give you his watch and chain, and diamond ring; and did you throw them overboard into the river?"

"No," said Boyington, "he did not give me his watch and chain and diamond ring, but was wearing them when I left him in the cemetery."

"You have heard officers testify that they saw you throw the watch and chain overboard. How do you explain that?"

"I had been eating an orange, and when the officers came upon the gangplank when the boat had been stopped between landings and looked up at me, I was just in the act of throwing the peelings overboard. They mistook these peelings for the watch and chain."

After Boyington had finished testifying, the case was closed. The solicitor, in his speech, pointed out the weakness of the testimony in behalf of the defense. He was surprised a man of Boyington's intelligence could not fix up a better story than the one he had told. He said Boyington went to the graveyard with Frost; came away without him; then tried to escape on the boat. His bowie knife did the deed. It was found at the point where he stabbed his partner and threw his body over the wall a few minutes later.

In Olcott's speech for the defense, he emphasized the fact that the very weakness of the defense was its strength. Would Boyington leave his own bowie knife near the body? He spoke directly to the jury saying that if Boyington had not been telling the truth, he would have fixed up a stronger case; that the entire case of the State against the defendant was wholly circumstantial. All the evidence and especially one link in it was very weak, and that link was in the fact that when the officers dragged the river, they did not find the watch and chain.

BOYINGTON was promptly found guilty and sentenced to hang. He appealed to the Supreme Court of Alabama on two technical exceptions which are thoroughly discussed in ALABAMA REPORTS, ANNOTATED EDITION, BOOK 6, PAGE 31—PORTER. At that time, they were forced to go to the Supreme Court on technical exceptions only and not on the merits of the case.

This great tribunal confirmed the decision of the lower court.

While waiting in jail for the day of his execution and after he realized there was no hope for him, he wrote many articles and poems in which he advised all young men to avoid gambling and drinking. He pointed out to them and explained how a life of sin and recklessness would bring its recompense of sorrows, heartaches and tears. His writings were smooth and very interesting.

He had been found guilty on November 22nd, 1834—six months and twelve days after the date of the crime. One week later Judge Chapman sentenced him to die on the gallows during the day of February 20th, 1835.

On the night of February 19th when every one had gone except the death watch, only a few hours before his execution, he wrote a letter to his best friend the Reverend Doctor W. T. Hamilton, the Presbyterian minister who had visited him daily. This letter clearly portrays the feeling of a healthy, vigorous, conscientious and innocent young man who fully realizes that he has but a few more hours to live. Boyington's letter follows:

My Dear, My Respected Friend:

I have raised my pen to address you, yet what shall I, what can I say to you? You have sat beside me in my lonely prison cell; I have listened to your kind, your generous counsel; you have been to me as a father; upon your bosom I have rested my burning brow, and your kindness has drawn from me tears such as nothing but sympathy like yours could have called forth. What think you must be the feelings that animate my heart toward you?

Do you, can you, will you believe me, the savage I have been represented? I can hardly write. Oh, that you would, that you could, see the inmost recesses of my heart. But I will—yes, I will be calm.

You have solemnly asked me whether I am guilty or innocent. The question itself implies a doubt; but I do not think it unkind. I have been a gay and a wild youth; I have been thoughtless; I have been guilty—guilty, but not guilty of Murder—not guilty of the crimes with which report has charged me.

I have not been a believer in the Doctrine of Christianity nor am I now (I regret to say it, for I know it will pain you); but from my earliest youth I have held my word when solemnly and sincerely pledged, as paramount to everything. It may sound like boasting—I know it will—but in the whole catalogue of the transactions of my life will not be found recorded a deliberate, intentional falsehood; and when I say upon my honor, by the love I bear to her who bore me, as I value your friendship, and as I hope for the happiness of my friends and vindication of my memory, I am. I am innocent of the murder of Nathaniel Frost. I swear it by the most solemn oaths that I consider binding.

Were I to tell the world I am guilty, who would doubt it? Not one. But when in the most solemn manner I declare my innocence, every ear, every heart is sealed. 'Tis hard, 'tis hard; but the day will, it must come when the stain will be removed. Aye, I repeat it. When I am no more in the land of the living, when my form shall have mouldered in the tomb, then sooner or later, the world will believe that they have wronged me. That thought—Oh, how consoling even now, when ere another day shall have passed, I shall be alike senseless of shame and approbation.

My dear sir, I must conclude, even what little I have written has been done with difficulty. While I feel more than volumes could express, I can only say, I thank, I respect, I honor you. May every blessing attend you, and when you would feel or say something sad, think or speak of—BOYINGTON.

At half past one on the afternoon of February 20th, 1835, the death parade was formed at the corner of Government and Royal Streets. The march was along Government Street for more than a mile to Bayou Street and then south to a vacant lot where the A. M. E. big Zion church now stands. This was before the days of electrocution and a gallows had been built on this ground.

Almost everybody in Mobile either joined the parade or lined the sidewalks of Government Street to watch the parade go by. A cart containing the coffin and drawn by a single black horse with Boyington and the Reverend Doctor Hamilton to whom the condemned man had written the letter quoted above, slowly walking behind it, formed the center of the procession. The prisoner was dressed in a black business suit and wore a stiff plug hat. He was not shackled in any way. As they passed along, Boyington would occasionally raise his hand to bid farewell to his friends as he recognized them.

When he reached the scaffold he mounted the thirteen steps without aid. A short prayer was spoken by Doctor Hamilton who, at its closing, turned to Boyington and said in a loud voice so all could hear: "Boyington, in a few minutes you will stand before your God. What is your last declaration?"

"I am innocent—I am innocent!" was the exclamation.

The minister then shook his hand, turned from him and walked down the steps.

Seeing his friend depart and now standing totally alone with his executioners, panic seized him. He sprang from the gallows on to the crowd that was packed thickly around it below him. So thick

The Scott Street Gate through which two of the principals in the Boyington case entered the cemetery. It was erected more than a century ago — in the year 1819

were the people and so sudden the move, that for a moment every one stood still as if petrified. Soon the officers were in action. Then began a foot race of death.

Because of his nine months in jail without exercise and the long walk to the place of execution, he had become weak. After breaking through the crowd, he could not run very fast, yet it took several officers some minutes to catch and subdue him.

WHEN he was finally lifted back to the trap door, the execution was bungled. Boyington died a most horrible death by strangulation. It was more than thirty minutes later that he was pronounced dead.

The body was buried in the northwest corner of the cemetery, the part the city had set aside for the poor. Later, some one planted, or there sprang from the grave a live oak. It has grown until it is a magnificent tree, today. (See photograph of this tree taken by the author, appearing on page 42).

Twenty-six years ago, that part of the cemetery was converted into a childrens' playground. No doubt, if Boyington could now know and feel the emotions of life and could listen to the happy laughter of children that every day run in play around the roots of the three under which he lies, there would be no heartache, nor would he feel like repeating the words of his last letter to his friend

"'Tis hard, 'tis hard . . . if you would feel or say something sad, think or speak of—BOYINGTON."

SIXTY YEARS LATER

IN September, 1894, the Honorable J. C. Richardson in a speech of summing up before a jury in Judge John R. Tyson's court in Haynsville, Alabama and in illustrating how strong circumstantial evidence may be mistaken, used the Boyington case as an illustration, relative to which he said:

"A number of years after the execution of Charles Boyington, Florence White sent for Mobile's chief of police. When he reached her, he found her very weak and almost in a dying condition. She had wasted away until she was a mere shadow of what she had once been. Her conscience, she said, had almost driven her crazy.

"With extreme effort, she reached under her pillow and took out a large gold watch and chain. On the chain was a fob and a diamond ring. She handed them to the chief who listened in awe to one of the most sordid stories that had ever been told in Alabama. She explained how 'her man' had secretly followed Frost and Boyington with a hope of robbing them. When he overheard them arrange to go to the cemetery where they could be alone, he had hurried to her and because he knew that Frost liked her and was very drunk, he persuaded her to go with him to the cemetery. They sneaked along the outside of the cemetery fence, watched their chance when the keeper was not looking and slipped in. They were quite positive that Boyington would leave Frost at the cemetery and it would be a big opportunity for them to take his money. They were successful in gaining entrance without being seen and hid among the evergreens near where the two friends sat and discussed her.

"As soon as Boyington had gone, she came out of hiding. It both surprised and pleased the somewhat intoxicated Frost.

"Her intention, she explained, was to rob him while he slept. He refused to lie down and with drunken perversity refused to sit down. With much enthusiasm he showed her the fine bowie knife Boyington had given him.

"Then because of some reckless demon in her, as well as the money she wanted, as her man who had moved around behind Frost hit him on the head with a club, she grabbed the knife and plunged it into his heart time after time, and Frost paid with his life for those hectic hours of debauchery and unwholesome living. They dragged his body over the wall and hid it in the bushes.

"She told the chief of police that 'her man' took the money, went on a spree and died with delirium tremens.

"It was not long after this that she died. The chief of police on leaving the interview with her, made a solemn oath never again to recommend conviction of a person purely on circumstantial evidence.

"The entire State of Alabama, as well as the rest of the country, was so shocked by the terrible tragedy Florence White's confession revealed that it brought a change in the criminal jurisprudence not only of Alabama, but also many other states. After that it was almost impos-

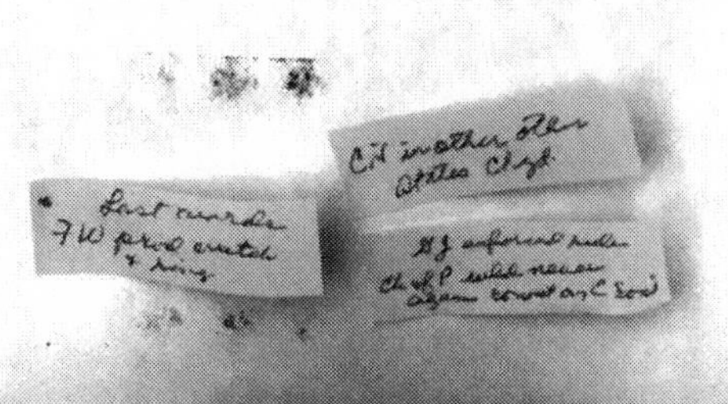

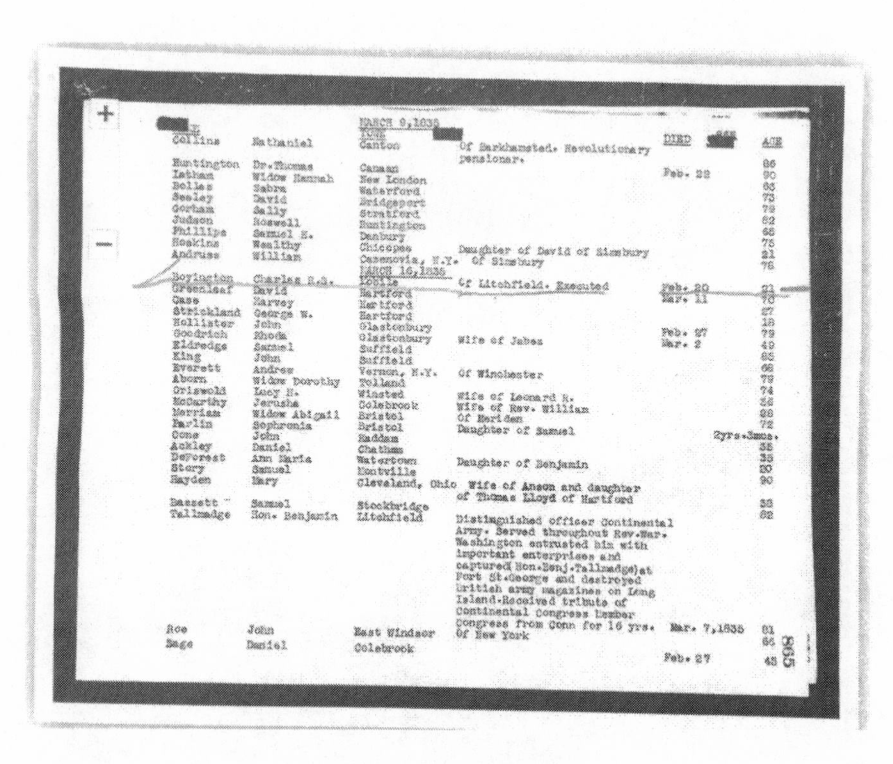

		MARCH 9,1836 TOWN		DIED	AGE
Collins	Nathaniel	Canton	Of Barkhamsted. Revolutionary pensioner.		
Huntington	Dr.Thomas	Canaan			86
Latham	Widow Hannah	New London		Feb. 22	90
Bolles	Sabra	Waterford			83
Seeley	David	Bridgeport			73
Gorham	Sally	Stratford			79
Judson	Roswell	Huntington			82
Phillips	Samuel H.	Danbury			68
Hoskins	Wealthy	Chicopee	Daughter of David of Simsbury		75
Andruss	William	Casenovia, N.Y.	Of Simsbury		21
					76
		MARCH 16,1836			
Boyington	Charles R.S.	Mobile	Of Litchfield. Executed	Feb. 20	21
Greenleaf	David	Hartford		Mar. 11	70
Case	Harvey	Hartford			27
Strickland	George W.	Hartford			18
Hollister	John	Glastonbury		Feb. 27	79
Goodrich	Rhoda	Glastonbury	Wife of Jabez	Mar. 2	49
Eldredge	Samuel	Suffield			85
King	John	Suffield			68
Everett	Andrew	Vernon, N.Y.	Of Winchester		79
Aborn	Widow Dorothy	Tolland			74
Griswold	Lucy H.	Winsted	Wife of Leonard R.		56
McCarthy	Jerusha	Colebrook	Wife of Rev. William		98
Merriam	Widow Abigail	Bristol	Of Meriden		72
Parlin	Sophronia	Bristol	Daughter of Samuel		2yrs.3mos.
Cone	John	Haddam			38
Ackley	Daniel	Chatham			33
DeForest	Ann Maria	Watertown	Daughter of Benjamin		20
Story	Samuel	Montville			90
Hayden	Mary	Cleveland, Ohio	Wife of Anson and daughter of Thomas Lloyd of Hartford		
Bassett	Samuel	Stockbridge			33
Tallmadge	Hon. Benjamin	Litchfield	Distinguished officer Continental Army. Served throughout Rev.War. Washington entrusted him with important enterprises and captured(Hon.Benj.Tallmadge)at Fort St.George and destroyed British army magazines on Long Island.Received tribute of Continental Congress Member Congress from Conn for 16 yrs.		82
Roe	John	East Windsor	Of New York	Mar. 7,1835	81
Sage	Daniel	Colebrook			86
				Feb. 27	43

Record of Death

Boyington's Poems

LINES WRITTEN ON HEARING OF THE DEATH OF MR. C. D. SOUTHWORTH AT SEA

Beneath the ocean's bounding waves
He rests his youthful head,
And the sea-nymphs, in their coral caves,
Sang their requiem o'er the dead.
No mourning friends stood 'round his bier,
As they launched him in the sea;
No funeral notes rang on the ear
But mermaids' melody.

He sleeps in youth and beauty soft,
He hath closed his short career,
But at his memory will oft
Fall friendship's crystal tear.
The heart that once with rapture throbbed
Is hushed within his breast,
Of its lustre, too, his eye is robbed
And his form has sunk to rest.

The monsters of the treacherous deep,

As they sport above his head

Shall pause to gaze where he doth sleep,

On his low, unguarded bed,

And tho' so soon his loss is felt

By friendship and by love,

And tho' he lies where sea-nymphs dwelt,

Yet his soul has gone above.

C. R. S. B.[1]

Mobile, Sept., 1834,

The Mobile Mercantile Advertiser.

Along with *My Mother's Blessing—At Parting,* it is suggested that *THE PRISONER* (Air—All's Well.) should be read as a lesson for all, especially young men. It was set to music by a Mobile lady, but it is unavailable.[2]

THE PRISONER

(Air—All's Well.)

From cell to cell echoes again

The clamoring of his ponderous chain;

The jailer opens his weary eyes,

And starting from his couch he cries

"Hark! Whence that sound?—Goodnight—All's well."

Weary with care and long confined,

The prisoner sleeps, while thro' his mind

Flits scenes of pleasure that were past

Before he felt misfortune's blast,

He joyous shouts, but wakes at last

To hear—he's safe—"Goodnight—All's well!"

City Prison, Mobile, Sept., 1834.[3]

LINES TO LIFE

Praise be to the God of the Universe!

Man's life is but a starry sky;

It lights up in brilliance for a while,

But being mortal it must die.

Oh, once again to walk in freedom,--

Free like the swallows in the sky—

And feel not these clanking fetters

That bind me into tearful cry.

Praise be to the God of the Universe!

I shall not doubt, but wonder why;

For looking back—oh! It would be useless,

For I am mortal and must die![4]

His references to God show signs that he may have questioned his own philosophy and is becoming more agnostic than atheist. It's a confusing stance for a proclaimed atheist. It causes readers to wonder: What does this young man really believe? Also, since he signs his name in different ways is he searching for his identity? Does Charles R.S. Boyington himself know who he really is?

THE INNOCENT VICTIM

(By C. R. S. Boyington, the Condemned.)

I love the glittering scenes of life—

The world's gay revelry!

Though brief have been my youthful days

They still are dear to me;

I love to gaze on beauty's smile,

And kiss her tears away;

I love to hear the soft breather words

Of thrilling poesy.

"Old nature's wild-wood loveliness,"
The forest, hill and dell
Are so dear, without a sigh,
To breathe a last farewell.
And still with rapture I behold
Creation's wonders, where
Each star stands glimmering in its sphere
Like islands of the air.

I love to pause and listen to
The murmuring of the sea,
The sighing breeze, the wood-bird's note,
All nature's mintrelsy.
And mid the haunts of early days
Doth memory fondly dwell,
And paint with varied colors bright
Each scene once known so well.

Methinks that now the merry laugh
Of schoolmates I can hear;
Each friendly voice of memory seems
Still ringing in my ear;
E'er now I see each maiden's blush,

Each smile of artless joy,
Each feature that I gazed upon
A happy thoughtless joy.

And ah! How true remembrance paints
One dear loved object there—
The bright eye, the lily cheek,
The rosebud in her hair.
Be still my heart—remembrance soon
Will sketch less faithfully,
And death the thrilling tumult hush
Through all eternity.

But oh! Most sadly dear is still
My mother's parting sigh,
Her last fond kiss, her soft embrace,
The bright tear in her eye;
And e'er till death will on my mind
Her words prophetic dwell:
"We may not meet again, my boy;
God bless thee—fare thee well!"

Yet though my mind calls up the past

To cheer the future view,

Soon must the world, the loved of life

Receive my last adieu.

The fearful words have been pronounced

That seal my earthly doom,

And with the spring's first flower will fade

My form within the tomb.

Before the destined day arrives

The anxious world will see

One effort for my absent friends,

One for my memory.

If I succeed, then I can say

With cheerful ecstacy, [sic]

"Oh death! Where is thy sting? I grave!

Where is thy victory?"

Mobile City Prison, 1835

"Executed February 1835,

W. L. W.[5]

The poems Boyington called *Jewels and Thoughts* have a slight difference in cadence and style. They are not as polished as his other works because he failed to revise them. However, the emotions in them made them worthy and popular enough that young men of that era, and even in the post-Civil War era, wrote in their girlfriends' autograph albums "a thought or two from Boyington".[6]

JEWELS AND THOUGHTS

I found a jewel

Shaped like a twenty-point star,

And in its center

A diamond shone with rare light

From afar.

On each point I read

A thought engraved thereon,

And as I held it up

Brighter and brighter it shone,

Until a voice

Came to me through the air,

And I answered back,

"Ho there! Ho There! Ho there![7]

MAN

Man is mortal and must die,

His is a gay laugh or sad sigh'

Man is like a bird,

His life is written in one word.

The good that man does in life

Comes out of labor, love and strife.

Earthly man can be

A jewel to life like a bee![8]

YOUTH AND AGE

A little child in its innocence

Knows not this world immense.

Determined youth, older people say,

Will remain young and strong always,

Yet in the end must pay.

Youth looks back with a smile,

Before him lies many a mile

Of both good and ill.

But youth holds not his thought,

Nor reminds himself of

Life's duties that must be wrought,

Nor does he know true love.

Beauty may cast its light on
A maiden's cheek of roses;
But fickleness and deceit
Compose her many poses.

When youth is gone
And age creeps on,
Man's life becomes a lore:
He looks back and says
"Nevermore!"

Yes, when the lightening
Strikes the tree of old,
Man stoops and bends
And strives for breath:
He may linger for a while,
But to him will surely come—
"Death!"[9]

FRIENDS

Friends are like the skies
That surround a bright star:

The star lights up the darkness

And makes the way clear and bright;

A friend while giving and loaning

Glitters with rays alluring;

But let the black clouds obscure

The stars bright rays,

A friend's friends drop off

And one by one they disappear;

For with a few exceptions, when man's money

Dwindles and his pockets are empty,

New friends are sought

And the old ones soon forgotten.[10]

MONEY

Money is the evil within
The palm of a man's hand:
If it is good money
Good and well will be bought with it;
But if it is ill-gotten money
The glitter on it will tarnish
Like the man who ill received it.[11]

GOLD

God is for shrines and temples
Where people kneel to pray:
If their prayer be good
The carats of its gold is pure,
But if their prayer be a curse
Its gold will lead to disaster.[12]

KINDNESS AND HATE

Kindness like hate
Rules the heart of man;
Sometimes its softens

Into sympathy and pity;

One thought from it

Will either give a helping hand,

Or cowardly strike to kill![13]

MAN AND WOMAN

Man is like a bat

While woman is like a butterfly;

A bat is keen and soars at night,

A woman lures man

Both day and night.[14]

THE HEART

The heart is but a pump,

Each throb is a cog

That pulls the blood back and forth;

Some hearts are kindly built

To relieve the suffering

Of the world.[15]

THE SOUL

If a man has a soul

The soul is the innerside

Of the shell they call his body;

And when nature calls him

From the ranks of other men,

Nature takes his soul in tow

And passes it out

Among the birds and flowers.[16]

SHYLOCK

Every man in this life

At one time or other

Has played Shylock:

Some Shylocks cheat the even scales,

While other lose the scales

Both weights and measures.

w *Charles R. S. Boyington*

City Prison, Sept. 20, 1834[17]

THE SENTENCED

They say the blest spring is here
With all her buds and flowers;
With singing birds and fountain clear,
Soft winds and sunny hours;
They say the earth looks new and bright,
That o'er the azure sky
The very clouds are fringed with light
And gaily floating by.

They tell me nature's full of life,
And man, of hope and joy;
But ah! Not so, my widowed wife,
My more than orphan boy!
For smiling nature cannot give
Such innocence as theirs
To me; nor can she bid me life
In answer to their prayers.

Beyond my dismal prison bars
The coy night air steals by;
And but a few pale trembling stars
Will greet my guilty eye.

Ere thrice the rising moon shall spread

Her mantle o'er the wave,

I shall be numbered with the dead

And fill a felon's grave.

To thee, alas! My noble son,

I leave a withered name—

A life, for all thy sire hath done

Of bitter, blighting shame!

And thou to whom I gave a love

More pure, and warm, and free,

Than e'er I placed on ought above—

What do I leave to thee?

A bleeding heart that cannot make

In throbbing pulses cease

That ever swells, but will not break—

A bosom robbed of peace!

A world all filled with prison gloom

By memory's cruel power:

Thou'lt smell the dungeon in the bloom

Of every vernal flower.

A pall will hang beside the way,

Boyington Oak: A Grave Injustice

Where e'er thy feet may go,

Upon the brightest path to lay

A shade of death and woe.

I leave thee as a tender vine

That felt the tempest rush,

And fell, with naught wheron to twine,

For every foot to crush!

These thoughts resistless, while I live,

Will careless anguish bring,

And in the last, sad moment give

To death a double sting.

From them, O Heaven! I turn to thee,

The sinner's friend to seek--.

If thou has pardoning grace for me,

O God! My pardon speak.

Thy spirit in the still small voice,

O, send with peace to mine;

And let this trembling soul rejoice

In being sealed as Thine!

Then through the world's dark wilderness,

Be thou the Widow's friend,

And let thy smile her visions bless,

Till life's sad journey end![18]

While in prison, Boyington wrote his own story of his arrest, trial and condemnation requesting that it be made public after his death. On February 23, 1835, following his hanging, The Mobile Mercantile Advertiser announced it was "offered for sale this morning at all the Book Stores in the place."

The pamphlet of forty pages was published "in compliance with Boyington's own request. He expressed the wish that proceeds from the net profit of book sales be forwarded to his mother and sister.

Only a small number were printed, so it was suggested that people wishing to purchase a copy "call early at the Book Stores." It sold for fifty cents.[19]

BOYINGTON!
AMAZING MYSTERY

Steam [illegible] of a century [illegible] twin craft to the [illegible] which Charles Boyington left Mobile, on May [illegible], 1834

Boat

his eyes like a frog on a lily pad. Frost and I rushed over to the rail and were watching him when a woman's voice behind us said:

"'The poor thing! And the water's so cold, too!' Nate seemed to become enamored of her at once. Of course, he

(*Above*) The spot where Nathaniel Frost was murdered, showing evergreens in which killer hid, and wall over which his body was dragged after the crime had been committed

"I have my suspicions," responded Boyington. "But I fear they will amount to nothing."

"Tell us in confidence," said Olcott.

"I'm almost ashamed to do so, but it is a woman. Her name is Florence White—a woman of doubtful reputation."

"Why do you suspect her? What reason do you have?"

"That's just the point. I have no reason whatsoever."

"WELL, there must be something to make you suspect she had a hand in the killing. Where did you first meet her?"

"We met her first after she came aboard our boat at Monroeville Landing on the way to Mobile. Perhaps I should start at the beginning. My parents are dead and I'm not yet twenty-one years old. I had a job last year on a plantation adjoining the one Frost owned south and west of Selma. We became the best of friends and when he shipped his cotton by boat to Mobile last fall, having saved up my money, I joined him on the trip down the river. We had a hilarious time together drinking and gambling for a week or two. When my money gave out, I signed as a sailor on the packet *Cubako*. Not caring for the life on the sea, after one trip to the Caribbean, I came back to Mobile and learned the art of printing."

"Go back," said Olcott, "to the time Florence White boarded your boat at Monroeville. Start from there and tell us everything that caused you to meet her and all that happened since."

"A very small incident," he said, "brought about our meeting. A cotton bale sliding down the skids from the top of the bluff struck some obstacle in its swift course. It began to change ends, and when it came into the lower deck

44

suspected the type of woman she was, but made the argument that we were out for a good time and no one would know the difference anyway. For the three days that we were coming down on the boat with her, she took up lots of his time, and when we were out on this spree in Mobile, we saw her every day. I could see that she was fleecing him and playing him for a sucker all the time. I never had any confidence in her, so Frost and myself fell out about her; she was the main topic of our last conversation in the cemetery. She is the only one I know in connection with him that I believe capable of committing murder for money," Boyington concluded.

Olcott asked: "Is that all you have that might be of use to us? If it is, it is certainly a slim beginning. However, I will employ a good man and see if we can dig up something."

That same day, a detective was hired and worked on the case for more than a week. He followed Florence White and found that she was living with a man who had spent a great deal of money for liquor, but who, at that time, was at the point of death with delirium tremens. No clue whatsoever

Frost Murder Site in Church Street Graveyard

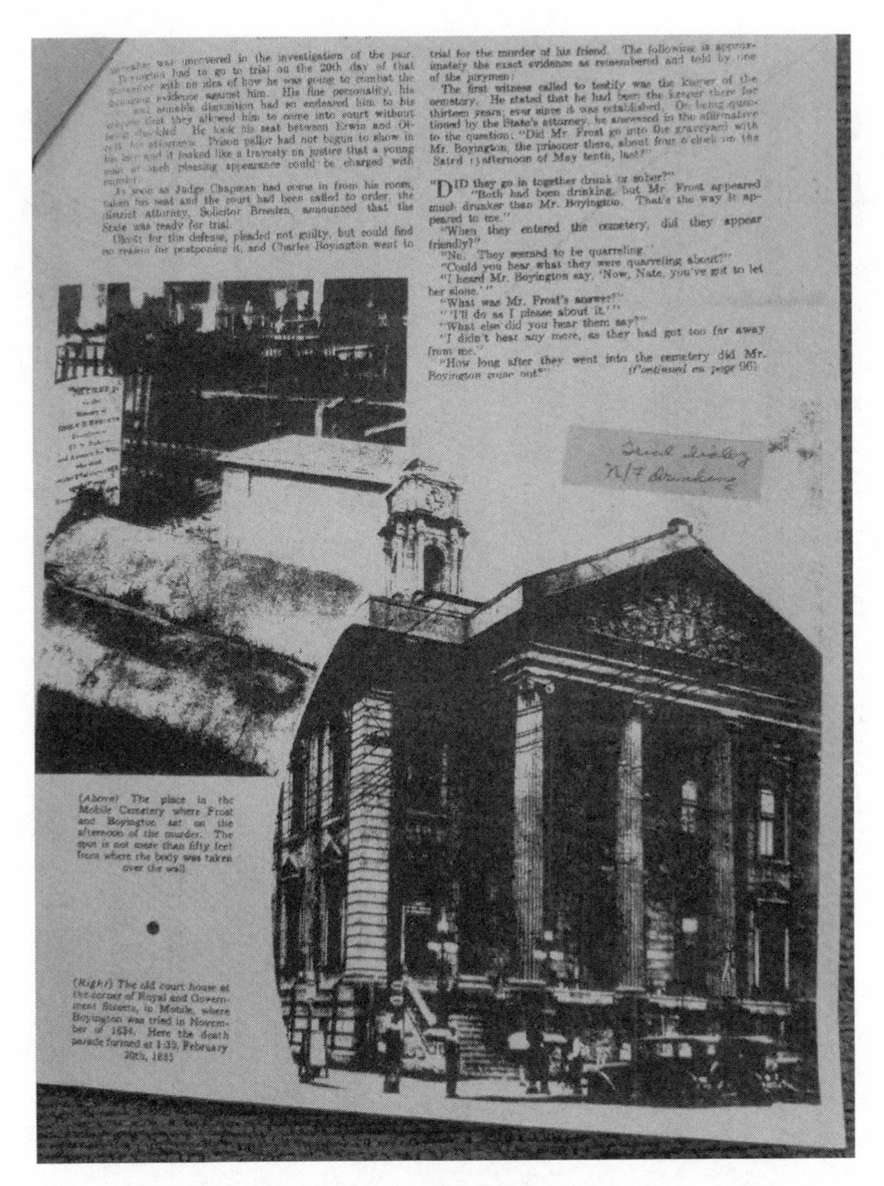

[illegible] was uncovered in the investigation of the pair. Boyington had to go to trial on the 20th day of that [illegible] with no idea of how he was going to combat the [illegible] evidence against him. His fine personality, his [illegible] and amiable disposition had so endeared him to his [illegible] that they allowed him to come into court without [illegible] shackled. He took his seat between Erwin and Ol[illegible] his attorneys. Prison pallor had not begun to show in [illegible] and it looked like a travesty on justice that a young man of such pleasing appearance could be charged with murder.

As soon as Judge Chapman had come in from his room, taken his seat and the court had been called to order, the district attorney, Solicitor Breeden, announced that the State was ready for trial.

Olcott for the defense, pleaded not guilty, but could find no reason for postponing it, and Charles Boyington went to trial for the murder of his friend. The following is approximately the exact evidence as remembered and told by one of the jurymen:

The first witness called to testify was the keeper of the cemetery. He stated that he had been the keeper there for thirteen years; ever since it was established. On being questioned by the State's attorney, he answered in the affirmative to the question: "Did Mr. Frost go into the graveyard with Mr. Boyington, the prisoner there, about four o'clock on the Saturday afternoon of May tenth, last?"

"DID they go in together drunk or sober?"

"Both had been drinking, but Mr. Frost appeared much drunker than Mr. Boyington. That's the way it appeared to me."

"When they entered the cemetery, did they appear friendly?"

"No. They seemed to be quarreling."

"Could you hear what they were quarreling about?"

"I heard Mr. Boyington say, 'Now, Nate, you've got to let her alone.'"

"What was Mr. Frost's answer?"

"'I'll do as I please about it.'"

"What else did you hear them say?"

"I didn't hear any more, as they had got too far away from me."

"How long after they went into the cemetery did Mr. Boyington come out?"

(Continued on page 96)

(Above) The place in the Mobile Cemetery where Frost and Boyington sat on the afternoon of the murder. The spot is not more than fifty feet from where the body was taken over the wall.

(Right) The old court house at the corner of Royal and Government Streets, in Mobile, where Boyington was tried in November of 1834. Here the death parade formed at 1:30, February 20th, 1835

(Top left) Church Street Graveyard (Bottom) Courthouse where trial was held and Death Procession formed there February 20, 1935

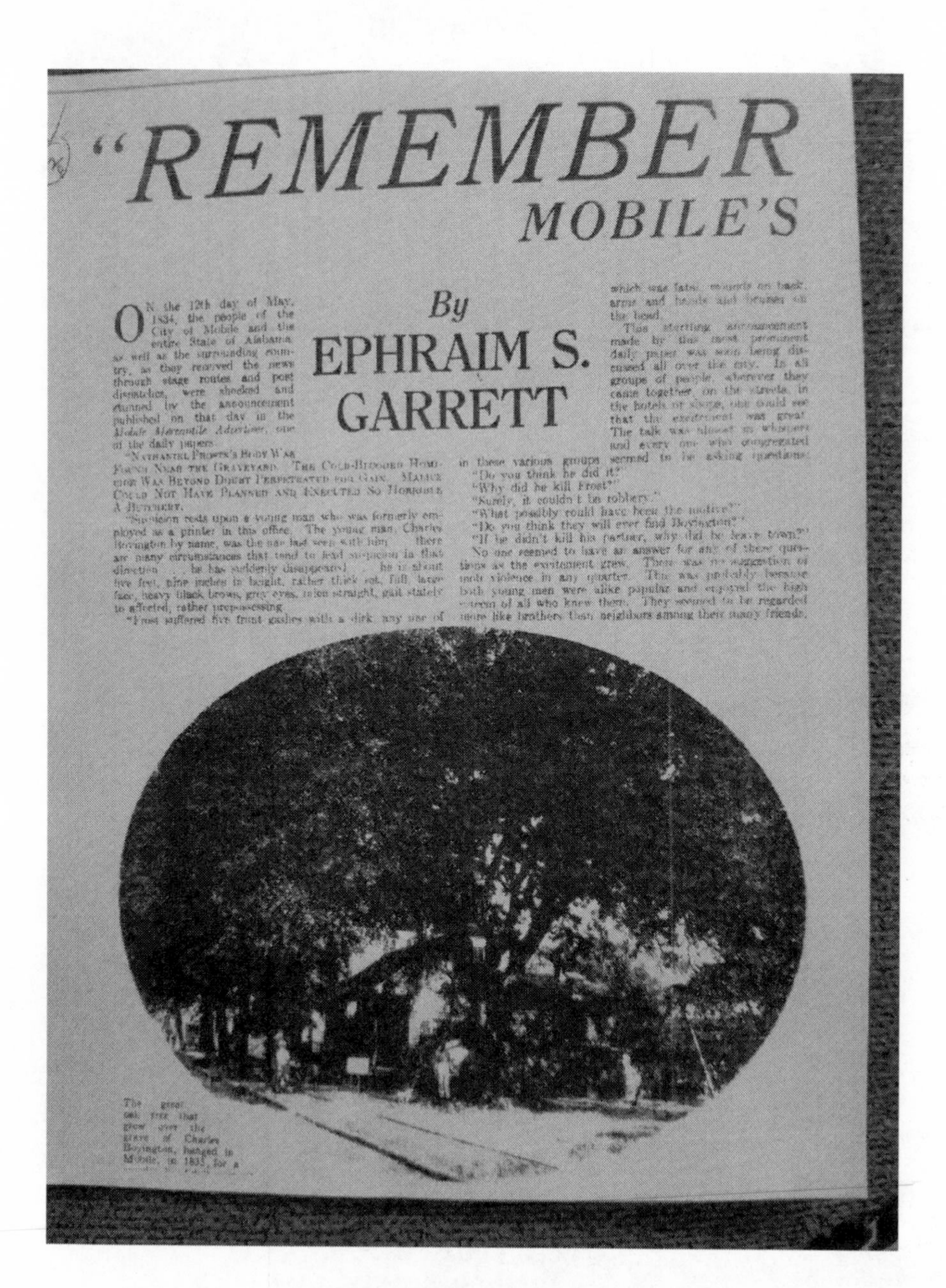

"REMEMBER MOBILE'S

By

EPHRAIM S. GARRETT

ON the 12th day of May, 1834, the people of the City of Mobile and the entire State of Alabama, as well as the surrounding country, as they received the news through stage routes and post dispatches, were shocked and stunned by the announcement published on that day in the *Mobile Mercantile Advertiser*, one of the daily papers:

"NATHANIEL FROST'S BODY WAS FOUND NEAR THE GRAVEYARD. THE COLD-BLOODED HOMICIDE WAS BEYOND DOUBT PERPETRATED FOR GAIN. MALICE COULD NOT HAVE PLANNED AND EXECUTED SO HORRIBLE A BUTCHERY.

"Suspicion rests upon a young man who was formerly employed as a printer in this office. The young man, Charles Boyington by name, was the [illegible] with him . . . there are many circumstances that tend to lead suspicion in that direction . . . he has suddenly disappeared . . . he is about five feet, nine inches in height, rather thick set, full large face, heavy black brows, grey eyes, nose straight, gait stately [illegible] affected, rather prepossessing.

"Frost suffered five front gashes with a dirk, any one of which was fatal, wounds on back, arms and hands and bruises on the head."

This startling announcement made by this most prominent daily paper was soon being discussed all over the city. In all groups of people, wherever they came together, on the streets, in the hotels or shops, one could see that the excitement was great. The talk was almost in whispers and every one who congregated in these various groups seemed to be asking questions:

"Do you think he did it?"

"Why did he kill Frost?"

"Surely, it couldn't be robbery."

"What possibly could have been the motive?"

"Do you think they will ever find Boyington?"

"If he didn't kill his partner, why did he leave town?"

No one seemed to have an answer for any of these questions as the excitement grew. There was no suggestion of mob violence in any quarter. This was probably because both young men were alike popular and enjoyed the high esteem of all who knew them. They seemed to be regarded more like brothers than neighbors among their many friends.

The great oak tree that grew over the grave of Charles Boyington, hanged in Mobile, in 1835, for a [illegible]

Remember Mobile

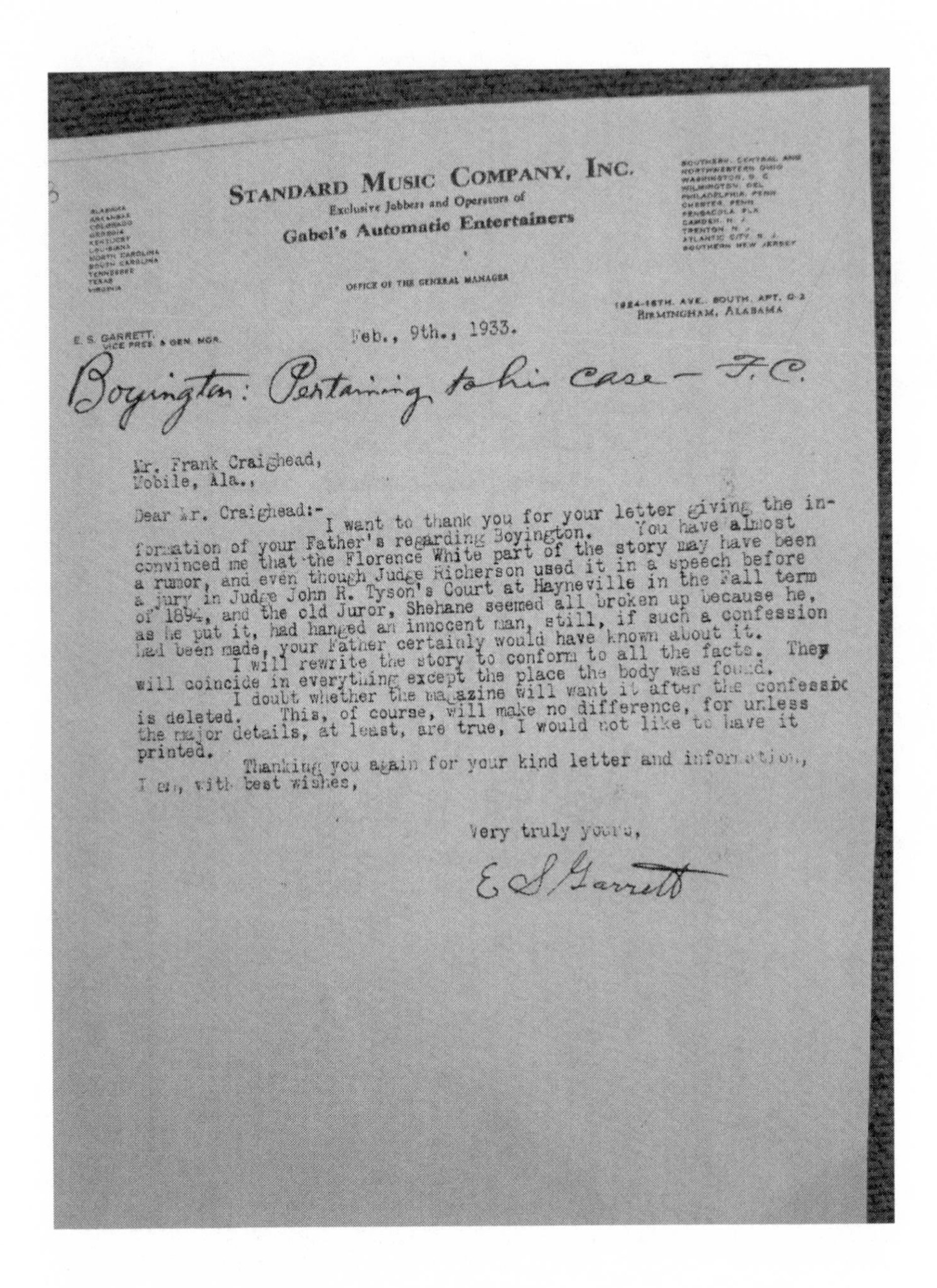

ALABAMA
ARKANSAS
COLORADO
GEORGIA
KENTUCKY
LOUISIANA
NORTH CAROLINA
SOUTH CAROLINA
TENNESSEE
TEXAS
VIRGINIA

STANDARD MUSIC COMPANY, INC.
Exclusive Jobbers and Operators of
Gabel's Automatic Entertainers

SOUTHERN, CENTRAL AND NORTHWESTERN OHIO
WASHINGTON, D. C.
WILMINGTON, DEL.
PHILADELPHIA, PENN.
CHESTER, PENN.
PENSACOLA, FLA.
CAMDEN, N. J.
TRENTON, N. J.
ATLANTIC CITY, N. J.
SOUTHERN NEW JERSEY

OFFICE OF THE GENERAL MANAGER

1924-16TH. AVE. SOUTH, APT. G-2
BIRMINGHAM, ALABAMA

E. S. GARRETT,
VICE PRES. & GEN. MGR.

Feb., 9th., 1933.

Boyington: Pertaining to his case — F. C.

Mr. Frank Craighead,
Mobile, Ala.,

Dear Mr. Craighead:-

I want to thank you for your letter giving the information of your Father's regarding Boyington. You have almost convinced me that the Florence White part of the story may have been a rumor, and even though Judge Richerson used it in a speech before a jury in Judge John R. Tyson's Court at Hayneville in the Fall term of 1894, and the old Juror, Shehane seemed all broken up because he, as he put it, had hanged an innocent man, still, if such a confession had been made, your Father certainly would have known about it.

I will rewrite the story to conform to all the facts. They will coincide in everything except the place the body was found.

I doubt whether the magazine will want it after the confession is deleted. This, of course, will make no difference, for unless the major details, at least, are true, I would not like to have it printed.

Thanking you again for your kind letter and information, I am, with best wishes,

Very truly yours,

E S Garrett

H

Boyington, Charles

Boyington, Charles R. S., defendant.
A Statement of the Trial of Charles
R. S. Boyington, who was indicted
and executed for the Murder of
Nathaniel Frost. Written by himself.
To which is added, a number
of fugitive pieces, in verse, also
written and composed by himself. Printed at the Office
of the Mercantile Advertiser, 1835
40 p. Title from McMurtrie.

Pg. 2 Col. 1 Mobile Commercial Register and Patriot

Tuesday May 13, 1834

There is a report in town, though we have been unable to trace it to any responsible source, that Boyington has been apprehended at Claiborne and confined in jail. It is said that an express from this city, with his description, reached Claiborne about an hour before the arrival of the steamboat James Monroe, which left here on Saturday evening, and that Boyington was found amon the passengers.

Execution Report

Mobile Mercantile A

May 17, 1834
page 2, col. 1

MOBILE:

SATURDAY, MAY 17, 1834.

Magistrates Court.—The hour set on yesterday for the trial of Boyington, arrested on suspicion of having murdered Nathaniel Frost, was ten o'clock, morning. From that time till near supper the magistrates court was occupied in taking testimony in relation to the charges, and the result of the investigation was a commitment for trial at the next Circuit Court. In the justice of this decision we do most cordially acquiesce, at the same time we cannot refrain from wondering, that not a syllable was uttered on this occasion, about admitting this unfortunate young man to bail—more especially as such a course is not without a precedent in this city.

We are indebted to our kind correspondents of the Charleston Courier for files of late N. York papers; from which we have gleaned several important items of foreign news for our columns to day. This liberal supply of intelligence from abroad, and the fact that the editor of this print and several of the workmen in the office were subpœnaed to attend the trial of Boyington yesterday, must be our apology for many omissions in our paper this morning.

Nothing of particular interest had transpired at Washington at our latest dates received.

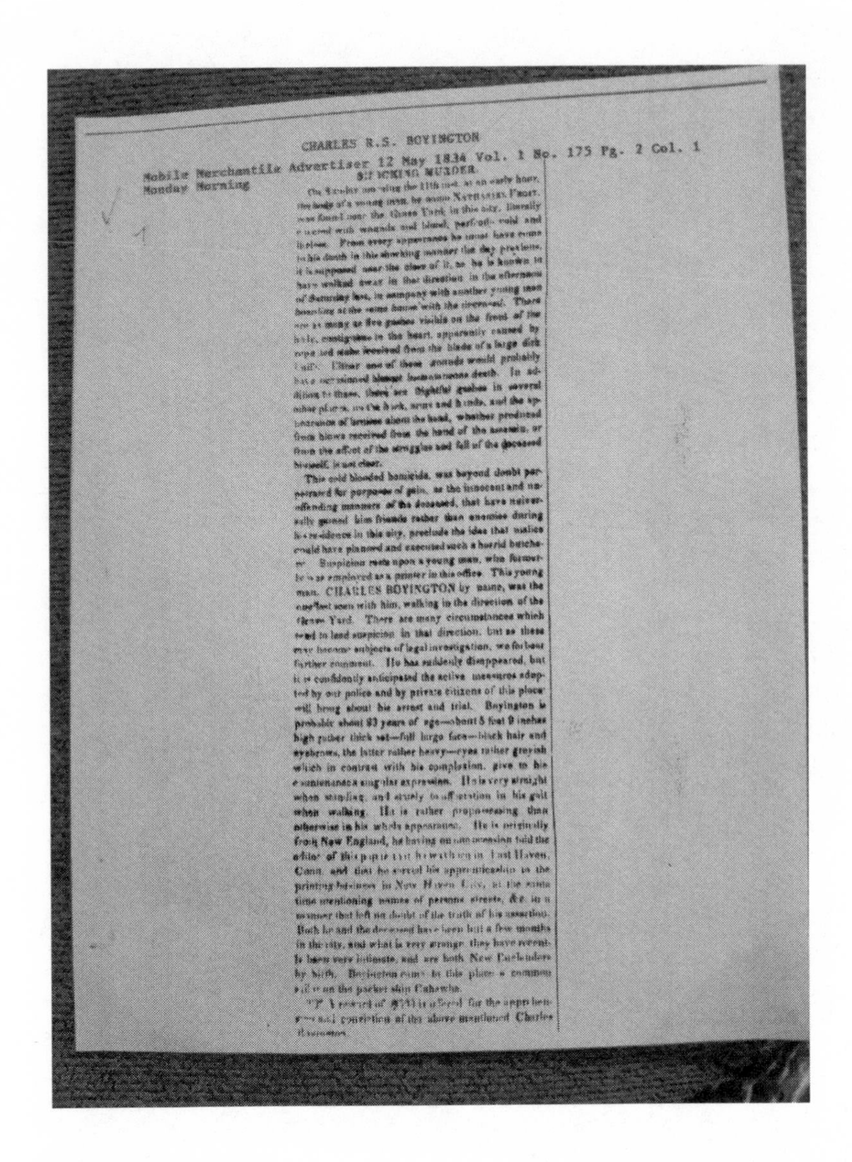

CHARLES R.S. BOYINGTON

Mobile Merchantile Advertiser 12 May 1834 Vol. 1 No. 175 Pg. 2 Col. 1
Monday Morning

SHOCKING MURDER.

On Sunday morning the 11th inst. at an early hour, the body of a young man, by name NATHANIEL FROST, was found near the Grave Yard in this city, literally covered with wounds and blood, perfectly cold and lifeless. From every appearance he must have come to his death in this shocking manner the day previous, it is supposed near the close of it, as he is known to have walked away in that direction in the afternoon of Saturday last, in company with another young man boarding at the same house with the deceased. There are as many as five gashes visible on the front of the body, contiguous to the heart, apparently caused by repeated stabs received from the blade of a large dirk knife. Either one of these wounds would probably have occasioned almost instantaneous death. In addition to these, there are frightful gashes in several other places, on the back, arms and hands, and the appearance of bruises about the head, whether produced from blows received from the hand of the assassin, or from the effect of the struggles and fall of the deceased himself, is not clear.

This cold blooded homicide, was beyond doubt perpetrated for purposes of gain, as the innocent and unoffending manners of the deceased, that have universally gained him friends rather than enemies during his residence in this city, preclude the idea that malice could have planned and executed such a horrid butchery. Suspicion rests upon a young man, who formerly was employed as a printer in this office. This young man, CHARLES BOYINGTON by name, was the one last seen with him, walking in the direction of the Grave Yard. There are many circumstances which tend to lead suspicion in that direction, but as these may become subjects of legal investigation, we forbear further comment. He has suddenly disappeared, but it is confidently anticipated the active measures adopted by our police and by private citizens of this place will bring about his arrest and trial. Boyington is probably about 23 years of age—about 5 feet 9 inches high rather thick set—full large face—black hair and eyebrows, the latter rather heavy—eyes rather greyish which in contrast with his complexion, give to his countenance a singular expression. He is very straight when standing, and strictly to affectation in his gait when walking. He is rather prepossessing than otherwise in his whole appearance. He is originally from New England, he having on one occasion told the editor of this paper that he was born in East Haven, Conn. and that he served his apprenticeship to the printing business in New Haven City, at the same time mentioning names of persons streets, &c. in a manner that left no doubt of the truth of his assertion. Both he and the deceased have been but a few months in the city, and what is very strange, they have recently been very intimate, and are both New Englanders by birth. Boyington came to this place a common sailor on the packet ship Cahawba.

☞ A reward of $[illegible] is offered for the apprehension and conviction of the above mentioned Charles Boyington.

FIFTEEN

REWARD OFFER AND ESCAPE

This editorial appeared in the Mobile Daily Register, May 11, 1834:

MURDER – The annals of crime have seldom been stained with a more diabolical act of atrocity than is our painful duty at this time to record. Early yesterday morning, the body of the young man by the name of Nathaniel Frost was discovered near the graveyard in this city. Shockingly cut and mangled...in a situation to leave no doubt that by... ...Barbarically assassinated. He was near the path where his remains were found. On Saturday afternoon in company with a young man by the name of Charles Boyington, and on whom suspicion strongly rests as the perpetrator of the horrid deed. The two boarded together at the same house. Bonington [sic] left the city precipitately on Saturday night; but from the prompt and energetic ... ... adopted by our city authorities and several public-spirited individuals for his apprehension. Wrong hopes are entertained and he may be overtaken and brought to trial. A description of his persona is given in a proclamation by the mayor, offering a reward of a like sum if he is convicted. Mr. Frost, we understand, is a native of New England, and came up to this city last fall. From unobtrusive and retiring manner he had formed by [sic] few acquaintances but he had gained the ... drem [sic] of all who knew him. Boyington is also a native a [sic] New England. He had cultivated the intimacy and friendship of Frost by acts of kindness and it appeared perpetuated the deed for the sake of plunder. (Reprinted in 1879 Mobile Daily Register-Reminiscences of Mobile[1])

The Mercantile Advertiser described Boyington in their editorial:

The said Boyington is a printer by trade about 23 years of age 5 feet 8 or nine inches high, of a dark complexion, dark hair, small dark eyes, with heave [sic] brown – of an imposing appearance – walked remarkedly straight. He came to this place about 5 months ago as a sailor on board the ship Cahaba, from New York, and said he had served his apprenticeship in New Haven, Conn. The object of the murder was probably plunder, as the pockets of the deceased were rifled of about fifty or sixty dollars, and also of a silver Lepine watch, with gold chased edge and second hand on the face.

When the body of the young man was found Sunday morning, it was literally covered with wounds and blood, perfectly cold and lifeless. From every appearance he must have come to his death in this shocking manner the day previous. There are as many as five gashes visible on the front of the body contiguous to the ear, apparently caused by the repeated stabs received from the blade of a large dirk knife. Either of these wounds would probably have coeasionsed almost in instantaneous death. In addition to these there are frightful gashes in several other places on the back, arms, and hands, and appearance of bruises about the head. Suspicion rests upon a young man, Charles Boyington, who was first employed as a printer in this office.[2]

Known facts about Charles Boyington's activities were scarce. According to his own report, about three p.m. on the afternoon of May 10, after leaving Nathaniel Frost, he returned to Royal Street to rent a horse. He claimed the one he'd asked for had "gone to the races," so he accepted another one and headed for Spring Hill. He didn't get far, though, before he found the horse moved too slow, so he returned it to the stable. He also bought two pistols for protection and made his way to catch a boat headed for Claiborne. From there, he planned to head North, eventually back to meet his family in New Haven.

It was spring; the temperature was in the seventies; by June, it could go as high as a hundred degrees. Leaving the sweltering weather was welcomed. But the hot temperature was the least of Charles' worries. He faced an entirely different type of *heat.*

About 3:30 that evening, Boyington returned to the boarding house alone. Other boarders—among whom were several printers who worked for the Mobile Commercial Register and Patriot and The Mobile Mercantile Advertiser—thought it strange to see him without his friend and "they ventured to ask where Frost was."[3]

He replied nonchalantly, "Oh, he is here somewhere; I am in a hurry, so I did not wait for him."

They noticed he appeared to be restless and worried, and he was also slightly pale.

"You took him walking," one of them said, "where is he?"

People knew that Frost was in very delicate health and was very weak, and knowing this fact, they were all of them anxious.[4]

Boyington answered in the same manner as before:

"Yes, and I brought him back."

His fellow printers noticed Boyington had become extremely nervous. One commented, "He tried to avoid everyone and hastily went to his and Frost's room, then a little latter [sic] just as hastily left the boarding house."[5]

His printer friends were surprised at his strange actions. He was seen later when he returned to Morris and Fraser's Livery Stable on St. Francis Street, where he'd hired the horse to go seven miles to Spring Hill. Next, he walked toward the wharves and spoke to several acquaintances, and that's when he purchased a pair of pistols and a dirk. About sunset, he went on board the steamboat James Monroe, which left the wharf about 8 p.m. for points north on the Alabama River.[6]

The next morning, Sunday, intense excitement and indignation pervaded the minds of the people when the announcement of the murder resounded through the press of the city.[7] It read as follows:

Proclamation to Mobile Newspapers May 12, 1834

MURDER.--$500 REWARD—City of Mobile upon the body of Nathaniel Frost; and whereas, suspicion rests on one Charles Boyington as the perpetrator of the horrid act; therefore, I john Stocking, Jr., Mayor of the City of Mobile, by virtue of authority in me vested by a special resolution of the Board of Aldermen, do hereby offer a reward of TWO HUNDRED and FIFTY DOLLARS in the event of the said Boyington being convicted of said murder.

JOHN STOCKING, JR

Mayor of Mobile

The above was posted in the Mobile Commercial Register and Patriot on Monday, May 12, 1834. It continued with a detailed description:

The said BOYINGTON is a printer by trade, about 23 years of age, 5 feet 8 or 9 inches high, of a dark complexion, dark hair, small dark eyes, with heavy brows of an imposing appearance walked remarkably strait. He wore a dark olive coat, dark satinett pantaloons, and a double-breasted silk velvet vest. He came to this place about 5 months ago, as a sailor on board the ship Cahaba, from New York, and said he had served his apprenticeship in New Haven, Connecticut. The object of the murder was probably plunder, as the pockets of the deceased were rifled of about fifty or sixty dollars, and also of a silver Lepine watch, with gold chased edge, and second hand on the face.[8]

At the time, Boyington planned to marry Rose de Fleur.[9] Mrs. George, Boyington's landlady, found a neatly wrapped package in his room. Inside, a note said to give the enclosed books, letters, and a miniature to his sweetheart.[10]

#

Whether he considered it an escape or not, Boyington headed out of Mobile. He boarded the James Monroe steamboat and was on his way. Soon, though, Boyington was recognized as a passenger. The acting postmaster at Claiborne, Al, sent a letter to Colonel H.H.B. Hays stating that Boyington had been identified as the boat docked in Claiborne. Also, someone said that the passenger had thrown a Lepine watch overboard.

That letter with the intelligence of the murder reached lawmen. As the *James Monroe* proceeded on it's way to Montgomery, Joseph Taylor and M. Dubois, officials of the law at Claiborne, rode horseback to head off the boat at Black's Bluff, 180 miles above Mobile, in order to apprehend him before he took the stagecoach for Georgia and was out of their reach. The lawmen succeeded in their quest by taking passage for Couton [sic]. On the way, they secured the prisoner and returned him to Claiborne.[11]

Upon being arrested, they searched Boyington, but much to their dismay, found nothing on him belonging to Frost. He did have $95 in notes and some silver pieces, which he never accounted for correctly His salary had been under $20 at one time, and he earned a total of around $100 from Pollard and Dade. From that, he had to pay for food, lodging, and other debts, some had been left unpaid. The speculation was that if Boyington had obtained this money honestly, he could have told how, but he never did.[12]

Nathaniel Frost is buried in the same cemetery where his body was found. His grave is unmarked, and its location is unknown. Frost's Obituary appeared in the Mobile Commercial Register and Patriot on Wednesday, May 14, 1834. It gave a glowing account of his life:

"The late Nathaniel Frost.- It seldom happens, while treading the rugged path of life, that we link to the chain of our acquaintance, a fellow being, possessing more sweetness of temper and urbanity of manner or high and enabling qualities of mind, than the' subject of this brief notice. Congeniality of hearts can exit, while human nature is the same, in but a very limited degree, but his retiring and unobtrusive habits, although not calculated to inspire friendship in every breast yet never failed to elicit esteem- and I am sure that the language of the poet will find a response in every heart:

'None knew him but to love him,

Nor named him but to praise.'

He came to this city about six months since from the State of Connecticut with the cherished hope that the gentle climate of the South would in a measure, deter the ravages of that withering, blight of the human family – consumption.

During the greater part of his residence here, he had been engaged in business, but finding that the application and attention required to his pursuits, were injurious to his health, and rather calculated to give an impetus to his disease, he had determined to abandon them, and for a week or two previous to his premature death, he had lived perfectly retired.

His relations and friends will have the consolation of knowing that on his arrival in this place, he was received into the social circle of a highly respectable family, from whom he experienced all the care and attention which the hand of kindness could bestow *and with whom he remained until his melancholy death.*

I cannot close this notice of one who has thus been buried by the hand of an assassin, to that "bourne from whence no travellor [sic] returns," without a passing remark upon the instability of human hopes. Indeed, the fairest flowers of earth are always the first to perish- and I never was more forcibly impressed with the correctness of the following line:-

Oh! How above Earth's fairest forms,

Death shakes his mildew'd wings;

And what a change a little time

Will make in human things."

M.[13]

This was one of the most horrendous murders in Mobile's history. The announcement of Boyington's arrest made May 15 was detailed. It said:

Arrest of Boyington.- We received positive intelligence this morning, that Boyington, the supposed murderer of Mr. Frost, has been taken.- A letter from the acting Post Master, at Claiborne, addressed to Col. H.H.R. Hays, states, that he was recognized among the passengers of the Steam Boat James Munroe, while she lay at the landing at that place, and that intelligence of the murder, with the circumstances attending it, reached there about three hours after the Boat had proceeded up the river. Mr. Joseph Taylor and Mr. M. Dubois, immediately started on horseback, with the view to head the Boat at Black's Bluff, and happily succeeded in their object. They took passage for Canton, and on their way up secured the prisoner, and returned him to Claiborne. We regret to add that he succeeded in throwing overboard the watch, which was relied upon as furnishing the connecting link in the chain of circumstantial evidence to establish his guilt. He may be expected here in the course of two or three days.[14] The Claiborne postmaster's letter connected the link in the chain of evidence to establish guilt.[15]

Another newspaper, the Mobile Mercantile Advertiser, objected to Boyington not being granted bail in an article published Saturday, May 17, 1834. It said:

Magistrate Court.—The hour set on yesterday for the trial of Boyington, arrested on suspicion of having murdered Nathaniel Frost, was ten o'clock, morning. From that time till near sunset the magistrates court was occupied. In taking testimony in relation to the charges, and the result of the investigation was a commitment for trial of the next Circuit Court. In the justice of this decision we do most cordially acquiesce, at the same time we cannot refrain from wondering that not a syllable was uttered on this occasion, about admitting this unfortunate young man to bail—more especially as such a course is not without a precedent.[16]

Two days later, they backed off and wrote the following apologetic article, which appeared in its May 19, 1834 issue:

In the hurried notice we gave on Saturday of Boyington's trial and commitment on the preceding day, we neither wished nor intended to cast any reflection on the gentlemen so assigned as counsel for the prisoner, very far from it. We had supposed our assertion that we assented most cordially to the decision of the court would have implied as much. In reference to this whole affair it may be said (and in the broadest and most exact unqualified terms too.) that both the publisher and the editor of this journal have been with the public in their feelings of astonishment and exasperation, at the act of butchery and outrage lately committed in this city. The excitement raised by such a deed of atrocity is an honest one, founded on the better feelings of human nature and on such principles of smart and heartfelt virtue as will secure the quiet of our houses and our firesides from the invasion of the murderer and shield our homes from the assassin's dagger. We glory in the manifestation of a quiet so comfortable to our citizens and so salutary to the peace and morals of the community. In so noticing the result of Boyington's trial an expression was used which we are free to confess was ironical in its intent and concerning which we would make the following explanatory remark—at the time we left the court house where the Magistrates Court had been in session with this case under investigation, the sentence of the Court had just been delivered, binding the prisoner over for farther trial. At the same instant almost the whole assembly within the Court room also left, under the same impression that we were, which was, that the proceedings were closed.. After that, we understand one of the gentlemen, counsel for the prisoner, made a motion that Boyington should be admitted to bail, for his appearance at the next term of court. There are perhaps hundreds as ignorant of the fact at this moment as we were on Saturday morning last at nine o'clock. All this however, is wide of the meaning intended by our remark on that subject in the last number of this journal. We have ever regarded it to an unusual indulgence for persons accused of capital offenses to be allowed to give bail sureties for their appearance at their final trial. The statute of this state, as of most others, expressly forbids such an allowance, except in cases where there is great doubt as to the guilt of the accused. That the remark previously made by us was ironical and was intended to make an allusion to the singular individual may be inferred from the references made to former procedures. That we intended to cast no reflection whatever on the Court, or on either gentlemen assigned as counsel for the prisoners, we must positively deny. Of the facts, and the additional ones that we did speak on during the trial and have spoken on since, in terms of the highest common fashion of the masterly manner in which the counsel for the accused managed the cases of their client, we are prepared to adduce unimpeachable testimony.[17]

#

The entire State of Alabama and the surrounding country were shocked when receiving news via stage routes and post dispatches that announced the cold-blooded homicide of Nathaniel Frost. They read in the Mobile Mercantile Advertiser about the man's body being found near the graveyard and that the murder was committed for gain, saying that "Malice Could Not Have Planned and Executed So Horrible a Butchery."[18]

It pointed to circumstances making Charles Boyington a suspect and the town was abuzz with discussion by stunned citizens. Speculation about motive and guilt abounded. The question, "If Boyington didn't kill his partner, why did he leave town?" kept being repeated. But no one had the answer.[19]

A huge crowd met the steamboat Courier when it arrived in Mobile from Montgomery Friday evening, May 16, 1834. Morbid and curious, they came to see Charles R.S. Boyington, the supposed murderer of Nathaniel Frost, who was onboard. Even slaves free for the day rushed to the cotton wharves to see "the young man charged with having imbued his hands in the blood of a kind friend," as officials escorted him to city prison at 104 Theatre Street, there was no disorder; no incident.

They entered the brick and mortar building that had no porch through cell doors into one of the four 6 by 9-foot rooms which housed four cells each. Brick floors two and a half feet deep allowed for settling. Slave labor probably made the bricks. Prisoners were on the downstairs level. The second floor was probably used for the court, and the third floor held offices for judges and lawyers. Barbed wire and broken glass bottles atop the outside wall prevented prisoners from escaping.[20]

Thrown into a dingy cell with other prisoners, Boyington wrinkled his nose at the stench of urine from a bucket and whiskey on the breath of drunken sailors singing off key at the top of their lungs. The mixed group included a couple of runaway slaves and a Negro woman trying to tend to her whimpering, naked baby.

He looked at the wall bunk, unlike the mattress in the boarding house he was accustomed to sleeping on which was reasonably comfortable. The cold, damp building had no fireplace, no bedding, no covering…as had been reported in the newspaper article about complaints: "This protest shows that the spirit of man was beginning to revolt against man's inhumanity as had been written about it in a protest headed *Horrors of the Jail* in its December issue, 1823 three years after the jail opened."[21]

He sat on the floor shivering and stared at the grill door closing the outer end through which came light and ventilation. Charles R.S. Boyington had never been in such a horrible, unbearable confinement. He stiffened. *I made it through that jail in New Haven; I can manage here.* He could stand it for one night, then he hoped to get bail.

Half an hour later, Boyington was taken to a private cell. He remained in irons all night.[22] As was the custom of the jails in Mobile at the time for an accused murderer, his feet would remain fettered to the wall with a short chain for the duration of his incarceration.

The following morning, he was conducted to the wood and brick Court House with its rear portion of undressed and unbarked pine logs on the southwest corner of Royal and Government Streets. In that building, referred to as The Log Court House, Boyington underwent a preliminary examination which continued from 10 a.m. until 6 p.m. He was fully committed for trial at the November term of the Circuit. The motion for bail was over.[23]

Charles Robert Stuart Boyington was no longer a free man.

SIXTEEN

BOYINGTON'S STORY

Charles had his own version of the happenings that resulted in his arrest. He led up to it by telling the history of his life in Mobile from the time he arrived on the ship Cahaba. He told about his employment with Messrs. Pollard & Dade saying he "left their employ, although never formally discharged."[1]

He then spoke of his acquaintance with George Williamson, a fellow-journeyman, telling how Williamson had become ill. Unemployed since April 1834, Charles was awaiting the time to be able to leave Mobile.

"So," he said, "I consented to become his room-mate and fellow-boarder, that, thereby, I might render him more effectual assistance in his illness, than I had previously done by occasional visits." further purported to be in debt and admitted he planned to leave Mobile, stating that he'd shown Williamson a map with a route he intended to take.[2]

Next, Charles told of his friendship with Frost saying, "We often sat, read, conversed and walked together…" and that Frost, an invalid, was frugal with his money.

Claiming the trip wasn't a sudden decision, Boyington said he'd plan to leave Mobile, but only for a while, and others knew about his intentions. He mentioned his main reason for the trip, a prearranged rendezvous with his mother in June at the home of his brother, Edwin, a clergyman in New York. When he received no response for his solicitations for money from northern friends and having debts in Mobile, Charles decided to wait no longer. So he left May 10, planning to take the route through Georgia which was the most expedient.[3]

Even though the stage office was close to the boarding house (others claimed it was to avoid being seen leaving) he rented a horse from the livery stable of Mr. Smith to go to Spring Hill. From there, he planned to send the horse back and take the stage to Portersville on the route to New Orleans.[4] Contradictions abounded. Boyington claimed he was at the stable three times and Smith said he came twice.[5]

Another incident happened between Black's Bluff and the residence of Mr. Johnson. Joseph Taylor (the lawman) offered to accept a bribe from Boyington for allowing his escape. After cautioning Boyington never to tell Dubois—who assisted in Boyington's arrest—Taylor said, "…You have got ninety-five dollars, and if you will give it to me I will find a way for you to go where you choose." Then he promised to give Boyington four or five dollars to enable him to leave the area.

Boyington replied, "Mr. Taylor, mark me; so far from fearing to go to Mobile on account of this alleged affair, I should rather seek an investigation than otherwise; but there are other circumstances connected with my affairs at Mobile that render me desirous of not returning there; and if you will give me twenty dollars and one of your horses to ride twenty or thirty miles, I will give you the remainder, which will be sixty-eight dollars—seven having been paid for my passage on board the boat."

At Taylor's request for more money, Boyington said he'd rather go to Mobile. Insistent, Taylor handed him the two pistols, saying he should pretend to be asleep. Then Taylor said he would "pretend to wake up and fire a pistol out the door."[6]

The agreement was never to tell if the plan failed. Even if it did, and Boyington went to trial, he wasn't worried. He knew several persons had been murdered in Mobile in the last ten months, but none of the accused was convicted.[7]Boyington kept insisting the money he'd had at the time of the murder was his, so Taylor moved on with another question, "...Did you kick a watch overboard?"

Boyington replied, "No sir, I kicked nothing overboard."

Taylor said, "I thought I heard something rattle like a gold chain, and so did some of the passengers; but I thought if it had been a watch the crystal would have broken." Despite claims of hearing "something jingling," no one saw the Lepine watch, nor shattered glass.

In an accounting regarding the money, it was reported that a man named Morrison swore: "a few days previous to the murder, in exchange for other money, I gave to Frost, in exchange for other money, a fifty dollar bill, on the *Bank of the State of Alabama*."[8]

The lawman had no proof of any of his suspicions. Also, if Taylor's bribe was a trick to get Boyington to appear guilty, it didn't work. The escape plan was never carried out.

Six months of being shackled to the wall most of the time might hinder Charles R.S. Boyington physically, but this scholar, musician, and poet held fast. He was so strong-willed, that being in this deplorable situation couldn't convince him he'd be convicted, stop his writing poetry, or break his spirit.

SEVENTEEN

BEHIND THE BARS

It may be hard for God-fearing people to understand how Charles survived in jail. As an atheist, he had no center to hold on to, and no God to pray to for help. One would think he existed in a hopeless situation. But he didn't. Somehow he managed to keep the thought that he would not be convicted. He continued writing poetry and managed to get it published, most likely because his writing was very eloquent. He was a literary genius.

He also had Rose. Despite her father's protests, she visited him as often as she could sneak away from home. She brought him flowers, fruits, and cakes.[1] In return, Charles' poetry illustrated his love for her. Her deep love for him helped him survive.

He wrote other poems, too. A month before the murder, he'd written one to his mother. Oddly enough, he mentioned God in a verse and in the accompanying letter to his mother, who had at least taught him there was a God.[2] That raises a question: Did Charles simply write what he knew his mother wanted to read, or was he the arch hypocrite? Perhaps this poem, published in The Mobile Mercantile Advertiser, April, 1834,[3] holds the answer:

MY MOTHER'S BLESSING—AT PARTING

Her cheek was pale, her dark eyes sad,

As she breathed her last farewell;

And oft she sighed, yet blessed the while

Her tears in sorrow fell.

Her lip, that quivered as she spoke,

Was like the lily's hue,

And high her heart did beat, as low

She signed a long adieu.

Warmly I pressed her trembling hand

"Farewell, dear Mother now,"

"God bless thee, boy"—her heart was full,

She kissed my burning brow.

A tear fell on my warm flushed cheek,

A Mother's tear of love:

"We soon must part," she said, "but we

Shall meet again above."

"When far hence, think oft, my son,

Of the days of youth and joy.

When all was happiness around,

Forget not these, my boy.

Remember then, how oft, in youth,

Thou'st rested on this breast,

And her who hath, in earlier days,

Thy infant form caress'd.

"Now go, be happy when afar,

But oh, do not forget

Thy mother, and they mother's love—

A parent's deep regret.

May heaven 'round thy youthful brow

Entwine its brightest wreath,

And send its blessing bounteously

With this, my farewell breath."[4]

Charles missed his family. Also, that was obvious during walks with Rose. Ironically, they'd pause to sit under the same chinquapin tree where Frost's body was later found, and Charles would often get into blue or melancholy spells and brood for his home and mother, and his brother and sister, back in Litchfield, Conn.

Sometimes Rose would cheer him up by telling him stories of the history of Mobile. "Mobile has been under four flags." She'd count them on her tiny fingers: "English, Spanish, French, and the U.S. Mobile has a great history, but it's a well-kept secret." She shook her index finger at him. “I bet you don’t know we became the cradle of the Carnival with a spontaneous celebration.”

“How?”

“Well, the first known Mardi Gras parade in 1711 by Mobile’s Boeuf Gras Society had sixteen men pulling a cart carrying a large papier-mache cow’s head.[5] I’m not sure about parades after that. But I know they were suspended in 1827 after a fire destroyed property from Mobile River to St. Emanuel Street to Government St.” She shook her head. “I was a child, but I remember it. It was awful.”

“I heard a little about that. So, when did they begin again?”

“In 1830. A tipsy cotton merchant and ship’s captain named Michael Krafft stumbled down the streets on New Year’s Eve. He and his merry band of revelers marched from the foot of Government Street off the pier--you know the one on Mobile’s Riverfront. They passed the warehouses, barrooms, and supply stores north of the French Fort making a racket with cowbells, and dragging rakes and hoes they’d, uh, ‘borrowed’ against wrought iron fences.” She giggled. “They awoke Mayor John Stocking.”

“Did he arrest them?”

She shook her head. “Oh, no. He invited them in for breakfast. That little escapade has turned into an annual event. They named the group the Cowbellion de Rakin Society.”

“I never heard of it. How do they classify it?”

“Sounds like it just may become the first mystic society in the world.”

By the end of Rose’s tale, Charles’ spirits lifted.

Changing her lover’s mood wasn’t as easy when Rose visited him in jail. In the squalor, it was difficult to be cheerful, but she managed. "Keep a positive thought, Charles Robert," she'd whisper through the bars. "They won't be able to prove anything. You'll be acquitted. I know you will. I prayed for you at Mass this morning. I have faith."

He'd slip his hand through the bars and intertwine their fingers. "Thank you, Rosa, my dear. I don't know what I'd do without you." Then he'd take out a poem written on a scrap of paper a guard gave him. "At least I can express my plight. I called this poem *The Prisoner's Song.*" He read:

'Tis morn!—The bright, the laughing morn"

The dew is sparkling on the lawn,

And gaily winds the "mellow horn,"

In the wildwood around;

The huntsmen with their voices cheer

Their steeds upon their wide career,

And 'fore the hounds the startled deer

Doth lightly spurn the sound.

Up comes the sun! Its cheering light

Dispels the dreary shades of night

And gilds the fields in beauty bright

Portending cloudless day;

While o'er the valley, hill and plain,

Waves like the sea the ripening grain,

And from each cliff echoes again.

The herdsman's joyous lay.

The bacchanalian's ceased his song,

And, parted from the giddy throng,

Homeward he wavering reels along,

Shrinking from public view.

The gallant from his mistress hies,

With fluttering heart and sparkling eyes—

But turning once again, he cries—

"My lady-love adieu!"

The bays' scarce ruffled by the gale

That sweeps from yonder verdant vale,

And freshening fills each loosen'd sail

That glides over the wave;

And on the far, far distant lea

The billows of the bounding sea—

The countless seamen's grave.

O! how I love, upon its tide,

Swiftly before the breeze to glide;

Now on its crest we seem to ride—

Now plunge into the deep\With "blue above the blue below,"

Trackless our course where'er we go—

I love to hear the ocean's flow

It's mountain surges sweep.

Boyington Oak: A Grave Injustice

The festive scene, and heedless thought

That fortune ne'er would shower aught

On me but happiness.

Ah! Little deemed I then to see

My days pass off thus lingeringly

As now, in my captivity,

Deprived of aught like bliss.

How now appear my boyhood's hours!

How false those scenes where 'neath green bowers

I culled the spring's first blooming flowers!

Those youthful pastimes seem

Delusive as a vision past,

That oft is o'er our slumbers cast,

And sad I feel, as when, at last,

We find 'tis but a dream.

Although upon my youthful breast

Adversity hath rudely prest,

Yet proudly I will stand the test

Tho' on my head suspicion's gale

Its fiercest blast hath blown.

On Justice's sword, so bright and sheen,

I look with and undaunted mein,

For 'twix us there doth intervene

An admantine shield:--

That shield is in my country's laws\And innocencee's unsullied cause,--

And seeking neither rest nor pause

I'm panting for the field..

And when the strife is o'er, farewell

To Southern shores; each hill and dell,

And Northern love shall echoing swell

The "rambler's" welcome home;

Each brother's voice I then shall hear—

Behold my sister, Mother dear,

And kiss away each falling tear—

No more from thence to roam.[6]

A tear trickled down Rose's cheek. She remembered him telling her about a hunting trip to Mon Louis Island as guests of the freed Creole-speaking yellow slave of the Baudin family and made a connection with the source.

She dried her eyes. "We all live on hope. That's beautiful, Charles."

"Did you see this in The Mobile Mercantile Advertiser on July 12,1834? Since my name has been conspicuously brought before the public, instead of my usual signature, I signed it *C.R.S. Boyington.* I'm elated that they published it." His eyes lit up. "I've talked to Pollard and Dade about publishing all of my poems as a part of my *Young Rambler's Folio* as soon as I have enough to make a volume in book form."[7]

"That would be wonderful." Se squeezed his hand. "It would be a gift to the world to share your talent."

The guard appeared at the door. "Time's up, Miss. You'll need to leave."

Rosa swallowed hard. "I love you." Frowning at the cockroach skittering by on the floor, she lifted her skirt and backed away from the bars separating them. "I'll visit again as soon as I can." She threw him a kiss as she exited the jail, cringing at the sight of the guard passing by her, entering the cell, and re-shackling her lover's legs and one wrist to the wall. How he could write, or even think, in such a situation was mind-boggling. Charles R.S. Boyington was a remarkable man.

Boyington had another visitor; oddly enough, one he sent for. The following day, Reverend William T. Hamilton, a newcomer who was a Presbyterian minister, made his first visit to Charles, an avowed atheist who, as a scholar, musician, and poet, denied God's very existence. Hamilton bypassed prisoners in the other fifteen cells in the four rooms and stopped at Charles' unit.[8]

"Good morning, Mr. Boyington," he said as the guard unlocked the door and provided him with a folding chair. "I am pleased that you requested to see me."

Boyington nodded. "I hope it's not an inconvenience."

"Oh, no. My church, the First Presbyterian Church, is just a few blocks walk. It's on the corner of Government and St. Emanuel Streets. I come here frequently to visit inmates since I moved to Mobile this year." His eyes lit up. "And it's a beautiful sunshiny day for a walk."

Boyington blinked. "And how I would love to bask in that sun."

"Oh, I am sorry." Hamilton shook his head. "I didn't mean…"

"Never mind. I am dealing with confinement." Charles turned to smile at the minister, "I welcome you to my abode, humble as it may be."

"Thank you, Mr. Boyington." When he saw he had the prisoner's full attention, he continued. "I have read some of your poetry, and I find it intriguing. I have heard that you claim to be an atheist." He leaned forward and placed his hand on top of a chain attached to Charles wrist and the wall. "But I find it difficult to believe a man so in touch with nature can deny God's existence."[9]

He received a blank look, so he continued. "Wouldn't you feel better if you told the truth regarding the murder? Perhaps it was an accident." No response. "Maybe the crime was committed in the heat of passion during an argument…"

"No," Boyington insisted in a loud voice, shaking the fist of his free hand. "I am innocent."

"Like all men, you have a soul worth saving. Your verses have soul in their words. Be honest with God. Be honest with me; then, I can help you. If you truly doubt that there is a God, tell me who prompts you to write such beautiful verse?"[10]

Boyington stiffened his shoulders as much as he could. "I will not confess to something I did not do. As for inspiration, nature is nature. It does not have to go beyond that."

Hamilton folded his hands and said the Lord's Prayer, but Charles did not even lower his head. Nor did he respond to the blessing the preacher bestowed on him. Silence.

However, as the minister rose to leave, Charles reached out to shake his hand. "Thank you for coming. I hope you will return soon and often."[11] But he didn't explain why he extended the invitation. His request remained a confusing contradiction.

EIGHTEEN

HEARING, INDICTMENT, SPIRITUAL ADVICE

During the hearing and indictment, the prisoner was in "a rack shack of a wood and brick building" on Royal and Government Streets, the Log Court House.[1] The elaborate preliminary examination, a custom in those days, began at ten a.m Saturday, May 17, 1834, and did not end until six p.m when Boyington was fully committed for trial at the November term of Circuit Court. The Counsel assigned to the prisoner asked for bail if Boyington could raise it, but that motion was overruled.[2]

One newspaper objected to that stance. The Saturday, May 17th issue of the Mobile Mercantile Advertiser article said:

Magistrates Court- Thour [sic] set on yesterday for the trial of Boyington, arrested on suspicion of having murdered Nathaniel Frost, was ten o'clock, morning. From this time until near sunset the magistrates court was occupied in taking testimony in relation to the charges, and the result of the investigation was a commitment for trial at the next Circuit Court. In the justice of this decision we do most cordially acquire, at the same time we cannon refrain from wondering, that not one syllable was uttered on this occasion, about admitting this unfortunate young man to bail- more especially as such a course is not without a precedent in this city.[3]

#

Although the Baron kept Rose under tight guard so she couldn't slip away to her fiancé, Reverend Hamilton faced no such restrictions. He visited as often as possible with his mission to extract a confession from the young man he'd made his charge, one he told others he felt duty-bound to prepare to meet his Maker.

On those visits, Boyington shared his poetry with the minister dedicated to saving his soul, the one he denied possessing. One day, he read aloud *The Prisoner's Song,* expressing his desolation in isolation, how he was not suppressed by fear or discouraged. He still had hope of not being executed. However, at the end, it ironically hints at resignation. Then he recited *The Tomb* with its symbol of earth and stone having "no stains," suggesting that he also had no stains and was not a murderer.

This provided Hamilton with an opening to bring up theological discussions—a chance to prove God's existence to the atheist. He first asked and received permission to speak frankly with the prisoner. In his lengthy sermon, Hamilton admitted that he had not been at Boyington's indictment hearing and claimed he was "entirely unprejudiced." He said that God knew the truth, and so did Boyington.

Referring to Jesus dying on the cross, the minister begged the prisoner to confess his sins to God, and man, saying, "If you are guilty of the crime charged against you, dismiss from your mind all hope of expectation of mercy in heaven or on earth unless you frankly confess your guilt." And he claimed that confession would provide relief, making a promise not to divulge anything without Boyington's permission.[4]

The preacher's words didn't sway Boyington. He calmly replied he had no confession to make. "I am not guilty of murder," he said in a normal tone of voice. He did admit to having other faults, then added, "…I am not a believer in the Christian system. I am not convinced of the existence of God."[5] *I'm listening to him and I'm being polite. Why can't he accept that I think differently? Don't we all have that right?*

Those words of denial of God's existence crushed Hamilton, especially coming from a man he admitted was "unusually intelligent, but had his belief fixed..." He questioned Boyington's early religious training. Although Hamilton didn't argue the point, saying he would not be rude, he queried Boyington's ideas saying, "Your conscience tells you that the grand objection you have against the Gospel is that it condemns you, and you are determined to disbelieve what, if true, must be so alarming to your fears." Then he asked, "How came you to adopt these sentiments?"

"Not from others, not from books, but chiefly from my own reflections," was the reply.

Hamilton retorted, "How then did everything around you come into existence?"

"I suppose things must always have been much as they are."

They bantered back and forth but neither budged. Finally, Hamilton conceded that he wasn't going to convince this doubter of the truth of God. The closest he came to impressing the prisoner was revealed with Boyington's inscrutable statement, "Well, kind friend...I think I must admit one cause for all things."[6]

Reverend Hamilton made many trips to the jail. He argued the point of God's existence saying God is like many other things that cannot be seen, nor heard, nor felt. "I cannot see justice, I cannot hear, nor handle, nor taste, nor smell it. How can I believe what is beyond the evidence of my senses?" After making that comparison, he turned to the issue of guilt. "And I will suppose that under the influence of these views, you, wanting money, and being acquainted with an individual who has some and whom from his known weakness of health, you suppose you can easily overpower, you entice him to go with you alone to a retired spot, and there, while he leans on your arm as on that of a known friend, you suddenly grasp that arm in your own and pierce him to the heart with repeated blows, rifle his pockets, and then looking around you and saying 'no eye sees me, no one can now impede my movements, this murdered friend can bring no charge.'"

He sighed. "You then walk away, leaving far behind you the bleeding corpse, the scene of your guilt and your clamorous creditors and when already scores of miles from the scene of this fiendish villainy, and while you are congratulating yourself on the success of your plans, suddenly you find yourself surrounded by strange faces, roughly accosted, charged with the guilt of murdering him you had left bleeding behind you—you are bound, searched, conducted back to the place from which you had fled…and the result is, here you are chained and fettered in this solitary cell awaiting the execution…" He then said, "Now, without deciding on the question of your personal guilt or innocence, is there no relevancy to the subject on which we have been conversing?"[7]

Eyes widened, Boyington replied, "I think there is."

Hamilton nodded. "You cannot see justice." His voice was a loud whisper. "…yet, this very principle of justice has arrested you." He added that a conviction would determine his fate and the judge would fix a date for the last day of his life. Next, he made a comparison to God's existence. "…you have ample evidence of the existence of God; and evidence, too, that He is powerful, intelligent and just; that He will punish sin wherever found, even though you can neither see Him, hear Him, nor touch Him."

Though Hamilton pressed the issue, it was obvious that Boyington's reply, "I must admit an intelligent cause as the origin of all things," was a sham.[8]

Still, Hamilton consoled the prisoner by saying justice should be tempered with mercy. "I come to offer you mercy from the eternal cause of all, through the death of Jesus, His Son, if you will sincerely repent and seek for mercy in His name. And you must admit Him to be wise and just, too."

Boyington countered, "Well, but that does not prove that Christianity is true, or that the soul is immortal."

Hamilton added, "Assured it does not, there is other proof for the truth of those points…But in your awful circumstances, it seems folly to waste time in mere argument. I come to offer you mercy from the eternal cause of all, through the death of Jesus, His Son, if you will sincerely repent and seek for mercy in His name."

Boyington took a deep breath. *He's telling me that mercy is conditional. I respect this man, but I can't agree with his philosophy, nor can I say that I do.* He stood his ground. "Your motives are kind I doubt not…but I do not believe in Christianity; I can not act or feel as if I did."[9]

With tears in his eyes, Hamilton pled with his charge, telling him he was deceiving himself and his calmness would not hold, that he'd counseled many infidels and only one kept his skepticism to the end and died "in cold contempt of religion."

He told Boyington it was "…not possible at your age you have as yet steeled your conscience so effectually."

In a controlled tone, Boyington replied, "I am sorry you think so of me. I cannot help it; and where I disbelieve, I am not mean enough to conceal it."

Trying to put the fear of God into him, the minister painted a gory description of his friend's upcoming execution, if he was condemned to "go to the gallows, probably as well in health, as active in intellect, and as capable of hope and of fear of self-approbation and of remorse, as at this very moment; as vigorous you will be in mind and body, when the noose is thrown around your neck, as you are now…your breath will stop, your heart will be still, your body dead! But can it be that this active mind of yours will there perish?—that it will be put out of being at once to be no more forever?...you cannot believe it!"

Taking a deep breath, he ended with, "Now what is there to show that the mind, or in other words the man himself, the soul will not be as entirely unhurt and unaltered by the pang which kills the body as it is by the process of fainting or by sleeping? The Gospel assures us that the soul will thus survive the body, and the resurrection of Jesus Christ from the dead proves it beyond the possibility of denial or rational doubt."[10]

Boyington raised his chin. "But I cannot believe the Bible!" he yelled.

Hamilton glared at him saying that he just wished it were untrue, and he gave several analogies and examples to prove his point, but Boyington insisted his beliefs, or lack thereof, were valid.

Unwilling to accept failure, the minister made a final plea: "Boyington, listen to me! Listen to one tenderly solicitous for your highest interests, and bow your knees in earnest prayer to the God of Mercy!"

The infidel fell to his knees and covered his face with his arm against his cell couch. Weakly, he replied, "I will try, sir." *I'm becoming a farce!*

Hamilton knelt beside him and said a prayer. He stood and gripped the young man's shoulder in a fatherly fashion. Walking out of the cell, he had a broad smile on his face, not knowing Boyington's tears were not of repentance, but because the minister reminded him of his mother scolding him for misbehavior when he was a child.[11]

NINETEEN

TRIAL

The trial had begun November 16, 1834. First-term Judge Samuel Chapman presided in the case of Charles R.S. Boyington for the murder of his friend Nathaniel Frost. Solicitor B.B. Breedin and James Dillet, Esq. represented the prosecution and Isaac H. Erwin and Edward Olcott, Esq. were counsel for the prisoner.[1]

Mobile citizens made the trial their universal topic of conversation; they were extremely interested. This vicious, cold-blooded murder was so horrible, and the accused so self-confident that from the time of the crime to the conviction people dealt with mixed emotions of repulsion and curiosity.[2]

Questioning began with Boyington's attorney, Edward R. Olcott, asking the accused if he suspected anyone else of the murder.

"I have my suspicions," Boyington replied. "But I fear they will amount to nothing." Acting ashamed to voice his thoughts, he named Florence White, calling her a "woman of doubtful reputation." Boyington claimed that Frost met her when she boarded their boat at Monroeville Landing on the way to Mobile.

Contradicting his statement that he left Mobile to visit his mother, Boyington said his parents were dead. He also admitted that he was not yet twenty-one-years-old. He changed his story about how he and Frost met, too. Few facts about this are available, but Boyington said he worked on a plantation adjoining one Frost owned near Selma and they became friends when Frost shipped his cotton by boat to Mobile the previous fall. He said the two of them "gambled and drank for a couple of weeks" until his money ran out. Then, Boyington claimed he signed on as a sailor and took one trip to the Caribbean. He didn't like that life, so he returned to Mobile and learned printing.[3] Previously, he'd said he'd learned his trade in New Haven. What to believe was questionable.

With prodding from Olcott, Boyington told of an incident when a cotton bale struck an obstacle, and the bale and the roustabout were thrown into the river. According to Boyington, as he and Frost watched, standing behind them Florence White expressed sympathy for the roustabout, and Frost was immediately enamored with the woman.

Boyington said his friend "suspected the type of woman she was, but made the argument that 'We were out for a good time and no one would know the difference anyway.'" He added, "she took up a lot of his time, and when we were out on this spree in Mobile, we saw her every day. I could see that she was fleecing him and playing him for a sucker all the time. I never had any confidence in her, so Frost and myself fell out about her; she was the topic of our last conversation in the cemetery. She is the only one I know in connection with him that I believe capable of committing murder for money."

Olcott hired a detective for a week. The man followed Florence White and found her living with a man "who had spent a great deal of money for liquor, but who, at that time, was at the point of death with delirium tremens. No clue whatsoever favorable to the plaintiff was uncovered in the investigation of the pair."

In the courtroom, Boyington sat between his two attorneys. Judge Samuel Chapman took his seat, and the court was called to order. The district attorney, Solicitor Breeden, announced that the State was ready for trial.

Aghast at the ghastly crime and curious about the details of the murder, people flocked to the Old Log Courthouse. The murder of Nathaniel Frost was a ghastly crime. They filed into the courtroom waiting to see the man who reportedly committed it, the man who had remained self-confident to the point of being unconcerned. He acted convinced that he'd be acquitted. The horror of it all caused excitement, which blended with curiosity."[4]

Accompanied by her chaperone Lydia, Rose entered, taking petit steps to her seat next to a friend. Using the lace-edged handkerchief she held in her hand, she wiped a tear from her eye as she sat on a long bench.[5] When her sweetheart was brought in by a guard, seeing him in shackles made her gasp. He looked pale and thin, and his jaw was set as if he were making a strong effort to control his feelings. He glanced in her direction, then looked away. She dabbed at her eyes, and Lydia patted her hand.

During the proceedings, the spectators remained solemn. It was shown that Frost's Lepine watch was missing, but part of the guard of the watch was left on the murdered man's clothes. Witnesses said when Boyington was arrested on the boat, they saw the accused make a sudden movement and "heard a jingling noise," and they thought Boyington was kicking the watch overboard. It was suggested that he'd had the timepiece on a string and dropped it down his pants leg into the water to avoid being caught with it on his person. Since nobody saw the watch, and no glass from breakage was found, this testimony did not count for much.[6]

Wisely, Boyington answered questions in as few words as possible. But he had a lot against him—no honest occupation, irregular habits, being the last person seen with Frost near the site of the murder, and leaving Mobile that same evening, plus having money he didn't account for in a satisfactory manner.[7]

Still, he managed to keep his emotions under control until his mother's name was mentioned. That reference brought tears to his eyes. He broke down and cried openly.[8]

The first witness, the keeper of the cemetery for thirteen years, since the graveyard was first established, was asked, "Did Mr. Frost go into the graveyard with Mr. Boyington, the prisoner there, about four o'clock on the afternoon of May tenth, last? Did they go in together drunk or sober?"

The reply was, "Both had been drinking but Mr. Frost appeared much drunker than Mr. Boyington. That's the way it appeared to me."

"When they entered the cemetery, did they appear friendly?"

"No. They seemed to be quarreling."

"Could you hear what they were quarreling about?"

"I heard Mr. Boyington say, 'Now, Nate, you've got to let her alone.'"

"What was Mr. Frost's answer?"

"'I'll do as I please about it.'" "What else did you hear them say?"

"I didn't hear nay more, as they had got too far away from em."[9]

The testimony by the cemetery keeper didn't seem to receive any consideration. No one questioned contradictions as to when, where, and how Boyington and Frost met, Boyington's claim that his parents were dead, where he served his apprenticeship as a printer, or the identity of Florence White and whether she might be involved in the murder. No follow-up was made.

Both sides presented their case. Despite Boyington's high hopes for dismissal, that never happened. The counsel for the prisoner summed up his case and it closed for the prosecution about midnight. The charge of the judge after retiring for an hour and a quarter was a guilty verdict on November 22. His Honor Judge Chapman passed upon Boyington on Saturday, November 29, 1834 "to be hung by the neck till dead on the 20th day of February 1835."[10]

Mobile County Sheriff T.L. Toulmin entered the information in the Book of Final Records in the Court House of Mobile County. It reads as follows:

"The State of Alabama Vs. Charles Boyington Indictment for Murder

This day the Prisoner being brought into Court by order of the presiding judge, B.B. Breedin, solicitor of the First Judicial Court of the State of Alabama, waves the Court for Judgment and sentence against him and it appearing that at a day of the present term of this Court the said Charles Boyington was found guilty in manner of form on charges of the said indictment and upon this it is asked by the Court bill of the said Charles Boyington if he hath or knows anything to say for himself why the court here ought not to proceed judgment and execution concerning him upon the said verdict,---who says nothing beside what at first he had said, whereupon all and singular the premises being seen and understood by the Court here it is considered by the Court here that the said Charles Boyington be taken hence to the common jail of Mobile County from whence he came, but be he there safely kept until Friday the 12th day of February next, and on that day be taken to some convenient place near the said jail between the hours of nine o'clock in the forenoon and four o'clock in the afternoon of the said twentieth day of February next be hanged by the neck until he be dead, and the sheriff of Mobile County is hereby charged with the execution of the Judgment and Sentence....

Record of Nov. 1834

T.L. Toulmin, Sheriff

An appeal was made on the fact that there was a misnomer in the indictment, "the right name being Charles R.S. Boyington" (the initials "R.S." had been left out), and also that an alien (a British citizen) served on the grand jury that brought in the indictment.[11] Non-citizens should not have been allowed to serve. The Supreme Court rejected both points.

In addition, one juror admitted being convinced Boyington was guilty. He said if the jury didn't convict, he'd kill Boyington himself, which should have disqualified him.[12] Boyington's attorneys neither protested nor attempted to strike that juror.

Much was written about the issues. First, Boyington pled in abatement of the indictment, claiming that his name was Charles R.S. Boyington and he'd been listed as Charles Boyington. The court struck out that plea.[13]

In OLCOTT, for Prisoner, Boyington's attorney said the court erred in striking out the plea in abatement. Referring to the rules of Criminal Law, he stated that the person must be convicted by the "finding of two juries: first, by the grand jury, who determines upon the guilt, in one point of view; and secondly, upon the finding of the petty jury, who establish that guilt in a more direct manner."

He argued that George Davis, jr, [sic] one juror who found the indictment "was not, at the time of such finding, a citizen of the United States-but, on the contrary, was a natural born subject of the King of Great Britain, and had never been naturalized." He quoted Coke saying "Aliens form cannot be returned of juries.[14]

He also stated that Chandler Waldo, another juror, expressed the opinion as to the guilt or innocence of the prisoner and should have been disqualified.

Olcott allowed some may argue that the grand jury members are accusers and they don't fix guilt, but he added that they can injure "a man of irreproachable character" and he called that an "odious offense."

Two objections stating the issues were brought up too late (after the indictment was found) was a mockery. Olcott cited various cases and reports to reinforce and validate his statements. One example was the ":...principle which actuated Chief Justice *Marshall,* in the trial of Aaron Burr, when he said 'this is the time" (before they were sworn.) 'when the accused has a right to take exceptions to the grand jurors.'" He claimed there should be exceptions to this ruling, and if there was a doubt as to how this should be handled, it should be in favor of the plea.[15]

Mr. Chief-Justice SAFFOLD took exception to Olcott's stand. On the fifteenth of November, 1834 (a day of the term of the Court), he said the plea regarding not using Boyington's middle initials was untrue. Two days later, Boyington filed two other pleas in abatement, claiming juror Davis was an alien and Waldo had formed an opinion regarding his guilt. Both were struck out as illegal and insufficient. On November 20, the prisoner had been arraigned, and he pled *not guilty.*[16]

During the trial, the presiding Judge reserved for the consideration of the Court, as novel and difficult, the question, whether or not an error in the decision of the Court, ordering the two pleas, as stated, to be stricken out."

Stafford stressed that the timing was off, saying "exceptions must be taken before indictment is found." He added, "By the statues of this state, these disqualifications are not expressed; it is only provided that, 'No person under the age of twenty one years, or above the age of sixty, nor any person continually sick, or who may be diseased at the time of the summons, nor any person who has been convicted of any felony, perjury, forgery, cheat, or conspiracy, or offence (*crimen falsi,*) shall be summoned on a jury." He also made the point that after an indictment, challenge to a juror serving was avoided because a juror was an alien. "Such an objection can only be made by challenging the juror before the trial," he said.[17]

Mr. Justice THORNTON agreed. He said disqualifying objections which affect the competency of a grand juror should not interfere.

Mr. Justice HITCHCOCK dissented. He refused to concur with the other judges' opinions, saying, "By the Common Law, these 'good and lawful men' must be citizens: they must not be 'aliens, villeins [sic], outlaws, either in criminal or personal actions…"

He added, "This statute does not embrace aliens, and no case can be found in England, where the question has been made." He referred to a case in England by 3d Henry VIII to prove his point and asked if U.S. law was "so guarded that no objections ought to be allowed after bill found?" He didn't think that seemed reasonable or just. He said, "By adopting the other rule, the act is made to sanctify the means, and the party loses his right to object, for not having done so before he had a motive, and on being arrested, though he can shew [sic] that the accusation has proceeded from aliens, felons and persons packed upon the jury by fraud, he is told that he is too late-the accusation has purified the accusers, and he cannot be heard. Even in a civil proceeding, a person is permitted to except to the illegality of a proceeding, until he waives the right; much more then should this right be held sacred in a criminal case, where it is said a man cannot waive his rights." Punctuating his claim, he said, "Indictments have been quashed, and *nolle prose qui's* have been entered for irregularities, much less than this. …be always pure, and the law can look crime in the face, and punish it without a blush." Eloquent as the words were, they didn't impress or impact the other justices. They voted against Boyington two to one. The ruling stood. The words were recorded as follows:

"Nov. 3, 1834. Page 158.[18]

Tuesday 4th November 1834. The court met pursuant to adjournment present as before.

"This morning after the Minutes of the Court of yesterday were read. Issac H. Erwin, Esq. an attorney of this court suggested to the Court that one of the members of the Grand Jury impaneled yesterday is not a citizen of the United States either by birth or naturalization – he also suggested that one other member of the said Grand Jury had expressed a sentiment so expressed was that if he was on the jury to try him (said Boyington) he would hang him – said I.H. Erwin Esq. accompanied the above suggestion with a remark that he was present on yesterday when the Grand Jury was impaneled and was apprised of the above facts but determined that he would not make the above suggestion at that time but at some subsequent period before any indictment found against Boyington."

Two years later, the Court reversed that precedent on a similar issue, but it was far too late to help Charles Boyington.[19]

The case against Charles R.S. Boyington's was very black, but this man, not yet 20 years of age, showed such talent in speaking and writing and acted so sincere in professing his innocence that some people cited his case as a miscarriage of justice, one decided on circumstantial evidence alone. It was important enough for Reverend Hamilton to write and publish an entire pamphlet on his conversations with the prisoner.

In it, he expressed his feelings and frustrations in a more or less objective style. Though his dedication to convert his charge never wavered, he had to admit he'd failed in his efforts.[20]

Nonetheless, the evidence was enough to convict. *GUILTY* was the verdict that was announced on November 22 at midnight. Execution was set for February 20, 1835. As they marched the prisoner away, with Lydia holding her up, Rose left the courtroom sobbing. She wasn't the only one crying. Few dry eyes were in the courtroom. Spectators, who'd come from far and near out of curiosity and awe at the horrible crime, wept at seeing such a talented teenager condemned to death. But there was nothing they could do.

The appeal based on a misnomer in the indictment regarding the correct name of Charles R.S. Boyington and the fact that a member of the grand jury was an alien went nowhere. The misnomer was deemed insignificant, and the point of law about the alien would have to have been brought up during the trial to be considered. Both points were refused by the supreme court.[21]

That cold day on November 22, 1834, matched the frozen heart of Charles Boyington, but it would warm up. He still had a statement to make. If that failed, he had hope that the Governor of the State of Alabama would intervene on his behalf at the last moment.

Boyington claimed his "sense of duty to my distant relatives and friends, and to my memory" was his main reason for writing this statement which he believed would satisfy "...every reasonable mind; and, in order that the readers may be able, without prejudice, to decide upon the success or failure of the attempt, I present the reasonable request, that, while perusing the following pages, they will entirely lay aside all the unfavorable impressions created by the verdict of the jury."

He concluded by saying:

"If, after having carefully examined all my arguments, you still believe me guilty, although I cannot but regret it, I shall submit to your decision;--but if you then consider me innocent, I confidently trust that there is no honorable man who will hesitate to acknowledge it."[22]

In those 30 pages, Boyington outlined his entire stay in Mobile beginning with his care of Mr. George Williamson, stating that he'd told his friend he intended to go North and showed him a pocket map of his route. He said he'd also read to George letters to his creditors, which he'd written because he was broke and unable to pay his bills. Those letters, including the date of his departure, were presented in court.

He next referred to meeting an invalid, Nathaniel Frost, who, like himself, was an unemployed printer at the time. Both visited with George Williamson at Captain William George's boarding house where they all lived. Of Frost's financial situation, all he knew was that Frost said the family of Captain George were his debtors. Frost also bragged that he had not "…squandered five dollars since he came to Mobile." He added that he'd "…never seen him have any money, whatsoever, or heard any person remark that he had.[23]"

Charles said his trip wasn't decided upon at the last minute. He wrote of planning months ahead to leave Mobile about the first of May to meet his mother in June at his brother's home. His brother, Edwin, was a clergyman in New York. The problem was that he didn't have the money to travel and nobody had come forward to provide it. Creditors were pressing him for payment. Finally, on May 10, he left to go to New Orleans, and then to New York. The cheapest route was by boat, but going on the Alabama River to Georgia (as he'd shown on the map to Mr. Williamson which was sworn to in court) was the route he eventually took.

However, the boarding house was near the stage office; if he left from there, people would notice. That's why he went to Smith's livery stable and rented a horse to go to Spring Hill. He intended to return on Sunday, send the horse back, and take the stage to Portersville on the route to New Orleans. He claimed this happened in the morning; in court, Smith testified it was in the evening around three-thirty or four p.m. He maintained those contradictions could be reconciled by the admission that he was at Smith's stable three times that day—once in the morning, once around three p.m. and again afterward. He said, "I must have been there *once before the races*…the races take place before noon." His point was that a person wouldn't rent a horse two hours before sunset to hire a horse to go to the races.

Oddly, he tempered his words by saying he wasn't questioning Mr. Smith's truthfulness, but that Smith was ill when he was taken from bed to testify. In compassion, he didn't want to keep the ailing man in court, so through his attorney, Boyington explained to Smith the mistake he made.[24]

Continuing, Boyington told of then returning to Captain George's house where he saw Mr. Frost and, before dinner, walked along Dauphin Street with him. They ate dinner at one-thirty, and he and Frost sat on the piazza and chatted about Mr. Williamson. About three-thirty, Frost went inside the house, and he decided to go to Spring Hill that evening instead of the next morning. It was then they decided to walk together until they parted and Boyington went down St. Emanuel Street, on Church Street. He arrived at Smith's stable on Royal Street before four o'clock. That's when he found out the horse he wanted had "gone to the races." He had no other saddle horses for rent.

Boyington left and returned to the boarding house, intending to leave the next day. However, he decided to try another place to rent a horse, and he headed for a stable on Dauphin Street, stopping on the way at Mr. Ballisette's Coffee House (sworn by Mr. Hilliard as happening earlier). He had no luck at the other stable.

Recalling some unfinished business with a Mr. Reuben Vail, he went up St. Lawrence Street and saw him (Vail also claimed that happened earlier). For the third time, he went to Smith's stable. Smith wasn't there, but he rented the white horse which he rode two blocks, but it was a rough ride, and he returned the horse right away.

At a third stable on St. Francis Street, no horse was available. On the way there, he saw Thomas Mills who testified to that fact in court. On Dauphin Street on his return, he spotted the steamboat James Monroe ready to depart and decided to take that route, the original one he'd shown to Williamson.

He stopped once on the way at the store of Messrs. Dunning & Knapp. Because he would be going through "a wild and unsettled country, which I was totally unacquainted, I resolved to purchase a pair of pistols, &cc., which I did (as sworn by Mr. Dunning.)"[25] Next, on the corner of Dauphin and Water Streets, he met fellow boarders, Messrs. James Ringwood and Hiram T. Henry, and he walked with them to Commerce Street (as sworn by them). He asked them if the steamboat was going to Montgomery and they said it was. He boarded the boat.

He next referred to the testimony of Mr. Wm. Moore, who said he saw Frost with walking westward arm-in-arm with Boyington on Dauphin Street near St. Emanuel Street on May 10 about three-thirty or four p.m. "In this testimony, Mr. M. is entirely wrong," he stated. Boyington claimed he and Frost "…never walked arm-in-arm" saying Frost was weak and he would not have leaned on him. "It would have been extremely improper…I was the smallest man…" He added, "it would have been equally unhandy for him to rest upon mine." He also questioned why they'd have gone down Dauphin Street if they were going to the graveyard. That route was out of the way and it was unlikely that they'd take it. He said that he and Frost weren't seen together within a mile of the site of his death—the graveyard.

He also disputed other testimony and that Wm. Henry George, eleven years old, swore Frost and Boyington were on his father's piazza about three-thirty and that Frost asked Boyington if he'd go to the graveyard and get blackberries. He said Boyington replied, "Yes," contradicting his father's testimony.

Mrs. Creighton, who was also on the piazza on the west side of the house at the time, swore before Judge Garrow and Justice Everett that she was sitting at a window on the south end of the boarding house when Frost and Boyington passed her. She said she asked Frost if they were going to pick blackberries. He said he'd go if she'd go with them. She refused.

Boyington questioned all the contradictions, asking who was to be believed. He pointed out that he could prove that he and Frost separated after they left Captain George's house, referring to Mr. John Caselle's sworn statement on May 10, 1834, saying at about three o'clock he saw Frost alone on Water Street. He was sure it was Frost as he knew him well. An affidavit was taken and sworn to by the witness. Unfortunately, this important fact wasn't communicated to Boyington's counsel until after the trial.

At nine p.m. on Monday evening, the James Monroe arrived at Black's Bluff forty-eight hours after leaving Mobile. It was a slow trip. They traveled only three and three-quarter miles per hour. Stepping out on the deck to smoke a cigar, Boyington saw a man running and shouting not to "pull off."

Unconcerned, Boyington went into the ladies' cabin and sat down watching a card game. He was taken aback when he felt a hand on his arm and discovered the man it belonged to held a pistol. (The hand turned out to be that of Mr. Joseph Taylor). Then he heard the words, "You are charged with murder."

He replied, "MURDER!" He claimed at the time he really didn't know what he was saying.

Men surrounded him and tied his hands behind him. They took his coat, vest, hat and boots, and several people checked them in the gentlemen's cabin. They found $95 in notes on the United States Bank and its branches, one $50 bill, one $5 bill, two $20 bills, and a pocket map. They claimed those items belonged to Frost. Boyington's having all that money was questionable because when he worked through the winter, some people said he never earned more than a hundred dollars. But Boyington said Pollard swore he'd paid him more than a hundred dollars at different times. He also claimed he'd won the money betting, but he couldn't prove it.

One point of contention concerned a *red bill.* Boyington reported that a man he thought was named Morrison said he'd given Frost such a bill, in the amount of $50, a few days before the murder. It was on the *Alabama Bank,* which had the back printed with red ink. Boyington asked what happened to it. He referred to Dunning swearing that when he bought the pistols, Dunning swore he only had $28, enough to pay for them. If he'd hidden it, why would he have chosen that one over the one on the United States Bank? He pointed out that, in Alabama, red bills are more common than United States Bank bills. Besides, he said, if he'd hidden anything, he would have hidden everything.

During that search, they thought Boyington dropped the watch overboard. Boyington claimed Taylor had startled him by putting "one of his hands in my pantaloons' pocket..." and that caused him to jerk, making it seem that he dropped a watch into the water.[26]

Boyington went with the authorities peacefully, but he declined to answer their questions. Charles knew his rights, and he said he later discovered his decision not to speak was a wise one "even for an innocent man."[27]

Yet, at the place for investigation, he still refused to respond to questions on the advice of his counsel. With Messrs. Taylor and Dubose, they left the steamboat Tuesday, May 13 in the morning. At Canton, they got a carriage and went to Black's Bluff to get horses and stopped at a Mr. Johnson's home for the night. Wednesday, they went to Claiborne and left there that evening. On Thursday at 8 p.m., they arrived in Mobile.

When they had an examination before Judge Garrow and Justice Everett, Boyington said Taylor gave a report of the arrest, and they talked about his attempted bribe. Taylor admitted to doubting whether the prisoner was guilty, so he offered to let him escape if he'd give him all the money he had. Boyington refused, but later said if he could keep $20, Taylor could keep the rest and they planned an escape. Still, Boyington claimed the money was his. Taylor promised Boyington "twenty dollars, *all his things,* and *a horse to ride."* He also said if the plan failed, the conversation would never go before a court of justice."[28]

Boyington knew if the case came before a jury, it would stress both the prosecuting attorney and his own counsel, so they asked him to write down the conversation word for word. In it, his plan was outlined. The scheme connected with Dubose, the other deputy. It said Boyington should not leave until late. "...Dubose has got all your money, and you must ask him to let you look at some of the papers in your pocket book; and when he takes it out, *I* will step up and take it out of *his* hand, and say *you* have no right to look at them. And then, when you go, you must take my pocket book too, to make it seem as if you robbed me of your pocket book at the same time."[29]

He promised to give Boyington time to escape and said, "...you must never hint that I helped you.- I am a tavern keeper and a jailor in Claiborne, and it would ruin me if it should become known."

Before the conversation was over, Boyington told Taylor, "...the money is mine..." he added that Taylor did not fear that the money would be recognized.

During that conversation, Boyington revealed why he wasn't worried. He said, "You say the affair has made a great deal of noise; but I suppose it will not be long before it will subside. There have been several persons killed in Mobile within the last eight or ten months, but I believe there has been no one convicted."

He was also convinced that by giving Taylor that money, he wouldn't be destitute. He'd have a horse, which he'd leave behind. But he would have had $20 and the pistols. When he reached Macon or Augusta in Georgia, he had friends who'd help him. In any event, he'd be out of the reach of his creditors.[30]

But the young man was wise beyond his years. He realized an innocent man would not be afraid of facing charges. Without knowing the particulars of the Mobile murder, he did know that having left there suddenly made him suspect and chased. He did expect letters he'd left to absolve him, even if he was not around.[31]

He also acknowledged that he had no wish to injure the character of Taylor, or anyone else. From experience, he'd learned that a blighted name is the "greatest ill that flesh is heir to." No doubt, someone had taught him good philosophy: that it is better to take a person's life than to crush his honor.[32]

An effort was made to prove Boyington's pocket book was Frost's but Frost's was red and his was dark green. They dropped the claim but while in prison, Boyington was told Frost's pocket book, &c., were found near his body, but nothing was brought into court. He thought the reason was, "Perhaps they might have told a tale too much in my favor."[33]

Committed to prison, he was shackled and chained in a way that forbade any exercise. Saying he wasn't trying to get sympathy from readers or recount his sufferings, he only wanted to establish his innocence. Then he added, "I might, it is true, paint a scene that humanity would shudder to look upon; I might represent a place

Which never echoed, but to sorrow's sounds,

The sign of long imprisonment, the step

If feet on which the iron clanked, the groan

Of death, the imprecation of despair!

"I might place before the mind's eye the inexorable walls, on which are traced

The names

Of my sad predecessors, in this place.

The dates of their despair, the brief words of

A grief too deep for many. Records that

Hold like an epitaph, their history;

Where the poor prisoner's tale is graven on

His dungeon barrier, like the lover's record

Upon the bark of some tall tree, which bears

His own and his beloved's name;

"I might, with an aching heart, describe my feelings, as, by the light which streams through the prison bars, I perused the epistles written by my friends afar; and I might delineate scenes to which these are but as a prologue—scenes beneath my parental roof—but it is no part of my design: before the inflictions of the law, however severe, I bow."[34]

Early on, during his confinement, Charles had written a letter to his family and friends It said:

My Dear Parents and Relatives:-

-I have a painful and terrible task to perform. It will require all the resolution that I possess to do it; it will wring my heart with the most bitter pangs; yet it must sooner or later be performed. It is to relate the results of the trial which I have lately undergone.—I know well that you have waited with painful anxiety to hear from me; you have opened this letter with hands trembling with suppressed emotion;--O! how fearfully, how terribly will that emotion be increased! In the various epistles that I have written since my arrest I have always spoken of my acquittal as a matter of course. In doing so I have never sought to excite hopes and anticipations that would be blasted by the result, for till the fearful moment when the verdict was pronounced; aye, even after the treacherous conduct of persons whom I had intended and endeavored to bring before the Court as witnesses, I had confidently imagined my discharge as certain.—Conscious of no guilt, I feared no condemnation. I placed myself, for trial, upon my country and God. I did it fearlessly, willingly. That country has pronounced me guilty. Mother, my dear and affectionate mother, it is to you more particularly that I would speak. You have nursed when an infant, you have watched my thoughtless hours of boyhood, you have seen me arrive at the stature and almost to the age of manhood; for twenty years nearly, you have known every action, almost every thought that has occupied me. I have never kept or sought to keep, anything whatsoever from your knowledge. Mother, have you ever found me a liar? Have you ever seen me scoff at sacred things? I am aware that you will unhesitatingly answer, no! Then by my veracity, by all I hold sacred upon the earth, by the great cause of all things, I swear that of the murder of Nathaniel Frost I am as innocent as a babe unborn; by word of deed I have never sought the life of any man.—You are my mother, and, knowing me, would have believed my assertions, without the formality of an oath; others may be less lenient, and therefore as it were, with one foot in my grave, at a time when I am about to

encounter the fearful mysteries of death, when I am about to say to you and to the world, farewell—perhaps forever, I have sworn my innocence. I know that the world will believe me guilty. I am conscious that no denial of mine, however solemn, will obviate that impression made upon the public mind by the verdict of the jury.—Fathers will read the story of my trial to their sons as a fearful warning; mothers will shudder at the mention of my name, and clasp their infants still more closely to their bosoms; I shall be called, I shall be believed a murderer.

It is hard to die, and although I have never seen a human being resign his breath, I know that his feelings at that trying moment must be awful, even though he dies believing he shall be blessed in after life, but oh—oh! To die upon a gallows and to be hung up like a dog, to be pointed at and derided, that, that is to [sic] much. But even that could have been borne, the self-consciousness of innocence could have supported me under any circumstances that might happen to me alone; yet I fear, I almost know that it will crush you, that it will destroy all your remaining happiness, and perhaps your life. Mother, hear me, remember what I say, for believing that you will do so is now my greatest consolation. I do not ask you not to grieve for me, for I know that such a request would be useless; but by all the love you bear me, by every tie that binds you to your other children and to your husband, I conjure you, conquer your bitter feelings. You are fast approaching the age when all who attain it must expect soon to die, and I pray you, whatever struggle it may cost, to quiet the anguish that my loss must create. Watch over the youth of my little sister, and let her caresses and affections solace your declining years. This is my earnest wish, my most earnest prayer.

To my step-father I can say but little. He has ever been kind to me; in his house I have been reared from infancy; he has watched over me and educated me with a father's care and a guardian's solicitude. That kindness I have but poorly, repaid, I acknowledge, and it is with pain that I confess it. I beg that he will pardon my disobedience and forget my errors.

Mary, watch over and comfort our mother, and receive my blessing. Edwin and Reuben, pardon the errors and folliew [follies?] of my youth, and believe that I have always felt toward you a brother's love.

My beloved friends, I have been occupied nearly all day in writing [sic] the preceding pages; for emotions, such as manhood and resolution vainly attempt to resist, have caused me often to pause.—But these feelings are not excited by fear. Death alone can never make me tremble, and probably no man lives who possesses a more absolute command over his mind and features than I do; in fact my personal appearance has been the subject of no little wonder, and some have called it hard-heartedness.

The real truth is this,--to the threats and sneers of a world I would not move a muscle or turn an eye—to the voice of reason, persuasion and friendship my feelings are alone susceptible, on an occasion like the present. Of these I have seen but little. My attorneys, Messrs. Isaac H. Erwin and Edward R. Olcott, have served me faithfully and kindly; they have been not only counselors, but friends—friends indeed, and when I saw them this morning it was in vain that I attempted to govern my emotions. I could not even thank them, though I know they will not think me ungrateful.

After having been brought into Court two or three times previously, on Thursday morning last, the trial commenced. It continued till Saturday morning at 2 o'clock. Had I been able to get all my witnesses, I believe that I should have been discharged; and, as it is, my kind attorneys will endeavor to get a hearlng before the Supreme Court; if that fails, a statement will be sent to the Governor for a reprieve, but with it goes no confession; I would sooner die than acknowledge a deed I never did. The proof was only circumstantial. I have not been sentenced. I will soon write again. Write to me. Be of good heart, my dear mother. Believe me innocent. Receive my best blessings.

Charles R.S. Boyington [35]

After being in prison six months, despite his claim that he would not be hanged, was Charles R. S. Boyington finally resigned to his fate, or was he simply ready to get it over with, no matter what the result?

TWENTY

LOOMING FATE

One year had passed since Charles first arrived in Mobile. How things had changed. Awaiting trial during the long summer and fall depressed him, but nothing like his current situation did. This year, Charles wouldn't attend the posh ball, nor would he be celebrating Christmas with Rose. Even as a non-believer in the birth of Christ, the spirit of the season was contagious. But he found it difficult, if not impossible, to be joyful all by himself. What did an atheist awaiting execution have to celebrate? He'd be alone on New Year's, too. If Rose did manage visits, they'd be brief and restricted.

The dark and dreary jail wasn't nearly as disconsolate as the way Charles felt. His heart filled with sorrow. Nobody from his family came to visit, not his mother, not his minister brother. Perhaps they couldn't afford the trip. His only escape was writing. Luckily, a couple of Mobilians who pitied him visited and, upon his request, they provided him with paper.

He wrote love letters to Rose; some have never been found. He also wrote many poems, which illustrated his literary genius. They were published, and blind poet and writer Thomas Cooper DeLeon recognized Boyington's talent. "They show that Boyington was a pronounced literary genius, even though his style differs in some of them," DeLeon said. Then he added a statement indicating that he thought the young man was guilty but under other circumstances the murder wouldn't have occurred: "He came of genteel people, and if he had been at home among his own people, he would not have lost his finer self and committed so terrible crime as he was accused of."[1]

After Boyington's death, the Editor Emeritus of The Mobile Register, Dr. Erwin Craighead, added to that praise. "With relation to Charles R. S. Boyington…he came into notice May 12, 1834, and departed this life February 20, 1835, his public career covering the short space of not quite nine months. It is nevertheless true that few persons have left so profound a mark upon their time as he; for there never has been for long a cessation of the discussion of what is known here as the Boyington Case. This young man was convicted upon circumstantial evidence of brutally slaying his most intimate friend Nathaniel Frost."

Craighead mentioned that, on appeal, the Supreme Court said, "he'd had a fair trial." He added that his earnestness in protest of innocence gained him sympathy and that "nothing in his previous life indicated the criminal."[2]

It was no secret that Boyington was well read and intelligent. Craighead said Hamilton was persuaded that Boyington was innocent. He then referred to a letter Boyington wrote saying it "…covered several large pages, all in the same elevated style and showing the same control over his feelings. Boyington was yet under age. The letter must be pronounced truly remarkable, from one so young and so situated…Good judgment in limiting his writing strictly to the matter in hand, firmness and conciseness of expression, elegant phraseology, and but not too deep sensibility, characterize it."[3] Heavy praise by a newspaper editor.

However, he had to undercut what he'd said about the minister's beliefs. "The minister lost confidence in Boyington's professions…The good doctor concluded that the whole conduct of Boyington was what we speak of now as camouflage, and artfully designed to excite sympathy and induce a pardon, at least a stay of execution. As it may have been that, or it may have been the last cry of an innocent soul, the debate goes on to this day: Was Boyington guilty? The question cannot be satisfactorily answered."[4] All had to acknowledge that whatever else he was, Charles Boyington was paradoxical.

Boyington had more to say on his own behalf. Continuing his statement using the light streaming through the prison bars, he expressed genuine concern for the judge, the prosecutors, his own attorneys, and the jailers. He spoke of being taken back to court on November 29, 1834, and listening to "an eloquent address, and what affected me still more, it was kind."[5]

He acknowledged that he wept at hearing his mother's name mentioned, but he didn't explain exactly why. Was it guilt, or sorrow at putting her through all of this, even though she wasn't present? He repeated the judge's words, *On Friday, the 20th day of February next, you shall be taken to some convenient place near the jail, and there be* HUNG BY THE NECK TILL YOU ARE DEAD—*may God have mercy on your soul.*[6]

The jailers received due notice from the man in shackles. "In speaking of my severe imprisonment," he wrote, "I think it is my duty to say, that, while every precaution for my safety has been taken, by the sheriff and officers in whose custody I have been placed, I have been treated with such kindness as not only calls forth from me the most sincere expressions of gratitude, but does honor to themselves and to humanity. The remembrance of it will be a bright spot in my gloomy tale."

He paid respect to the prosecutors. "Although a prison is but a poor place for complimentary remarks," he said, "I feel myself obliged to express my thanks to the prosecuting officer for the manner in which he has conducted the case, and, more particularly, for the kindness he has evinced, since the trial, in tendering for my inspection, the evidence given upon the first examination, and other papers, in his passion. For the faithful discharge of their duty, I could never feel, toward him or any other individual, ungenerous sentiments."[7] That's an unusual stance for a condemned man to say the least.

He mentioned that key witnesses were absent at the trial, including Mr. Williamson, Mrs. Creighton, Captain George and Mr. Morrison. He excused his attorneys for not forcing their appearance saying, "I think it is my duty to my kind attorneys to state, that the absent witnesses, of whom I have spoken, were all, I believe, beyond the jurisdiction of the court, and, therefore, could not be compelled to appear, although every exertion was made, both by my counsel and myself, to obtain them."[8]

He also expressed outrage at being accused of murdering his friend. "This is the unkindest cut of all," he said, "I will not insult myself by asking those who know me if they believe it."

In reference to his job, he claimed he'd never been formally discharged and that his job as a printer was a lucrative one. He added that he was not in dire straits, nor pressed to stay in Mobile and that he could have obtained employment in New Orleans at a higher salary. He even said his employers would have helped him if he'd asked for their assistance. So, he claimed no need to resort to the "dishonest means to obtain that for which, it is said, I slew my friend." He asked readers, "—do you believe me an idiot? Do you think me a lunatic?" He asked whether people thought he would have come back to the city where the murder took place "in the suburbs of which the body was still warm…hire a fleet horse…then, with the heart's blood of the corpse still reeking upon my hands, return that horse merely because he had not an easy gate?"[9]

He admitted that "…no mere assertion of mine, delivered under any circumstances, however solemn, will erase the impression created, by the verdict of the jury, upon the public mind, but when my assertions are supported by the most positive proof: when that proof is entirely noncontradicted [sic], and when my statement is, in no way, inconsistent with that verdict, then, I claim my words are to be credited."

Turning poetic, he added, "When the luxuriance of Spring shall deck the garden of Nature, and all creation rejoice in its beauties, where shall I be? My form will be, like a flower of a season past, broken and withered! The wild rose may bloom upon my dishonorable grave, but its fragrance will be unknown and its beauty unmarked by me; dust will have returned to dust, ashes to ashes. Death will have been encountered, its mystery revealed, and I shall be—what?"[10] *I don't know what lies ahead. Is it nothing? I can't even guess what it may be.*

He then referenced religion, still maintaining his atheistic stance, but claiming to have investigated Christianity both before and during his imprisonment. He said he'd been a high-spirited youth, but not a thoughtless one. Perhaps he had a humanitarian attitude. In his short life, he said he'd enjoyed many adventures and much misfortune. His schoolmates, he said, would know he had "bright pictures of hope and expectation," and his wish was that they'd never believe he was guilty that, "…should the design for which this epistle is being written be attained, and the world believe me, as I am, innocent, death will be, in no slight degree, deprived of its sting and the grave of."[11]

It ended, "Let those who will have read what I have written, candidly examine the facts that I have proved as well as asserted, then decide whether I have or have not proved my innocence, and let the opinion formed *after* that examination govern their language when they speak of me"[12]

He managed to get his work to the newspapers; Reverend Hamilton may have been the errand boy. At any rate, they published his poems and Mobilians read them. Some were romantic; others reflected his plight. All seemed to evoke emotion from readers. These two illustrate his state of mind:

For the Mercantile Advertiser.

THE PRISONER

Air—"All's Well.:

From cell to cell echoes again

The clanking of his ponderous chain;

The jailor opes his weary eyes,

And, starting from his couch, he cries,

Hark!—whence that sound?—good night—all's well,

Weary with care and long confined,

The prisoner sleeps, while thro' his mind

Flit scenes of pleasure that were past

Before he felt misfortune's blast;

He joyous shouts, but wakes at last

To hear—he's safe—good night—all's well.

C. R. S. B.

City Prison, Mobile, Sept. 1834[13]

The other:

For the Mercantile Advertiser

LINES

By the condemned

I love the glitt'ring scenes of life,
The world's gay revelry;
Though brief have been my youthful days,
They still are dear to me.
I love to gaze on beauty's smile,
And kiss her tears away;
I love to hear the soft breathed words
Of thrilling poesy.

"Old nature's wild wood loveliness,"
The forest, hill, and dell,
Are all too dear, without a sigh,
To breathe a last farewell;
And still with rapture, I behold
Creation's wonders, where
Each star stands glimm'ring in its sphere
Like islands of the air.

Mary S Palmer

I love to pause, and listen to

The murm'ring of the sea'

The sighing breeze, the wood bird's note,

All nature's minstrelsy;

And 'mid the haunts of early days

Doth mem'ry fondly dwell,

And paint, with varied colors bright,

Each scene once known so well.

Methinks that now the merry laugh

Of schoolmates I can hear;

Each friendly voice to mem'ry seems

Still ringing in my ear.

E'en now I see each maiden's blush,

Each smile of artless joy,

Each feature that I gazed upon,

A happy, thoughtless boy.

And, ah, how true remembrance paints

One dear loved object there,--

The bright blue eye, the lily cheek,

The rose-bud in her hair,--

(Be still, my heart, remembrance soon

Will sketch less faithfully,

And death they thrilling tumult hush

Through all eternity.)

But oh! Most sadly dear is still

My mother's parting sigh,

Her last fond kiss, her soft embrace,

The bright tear in her eye;

And e're till death, will, on my mind,

Her words prophetic dwell—

"We may not meet again, my boy,

God bless thee,--fare thee well!"

Yet, though my mind calls up the past,

To cheer the future view,

Soon must the world, the loved of life,

Receive my last adieu;

The fearful words have been pronounced,

That seal my earthly doom,

And with the spring's first flowers, will fade

My form within the tomb.

But ere the destined day arrives,

The anxious world shall see

One effort for my distant friends—

Ine for my memory.

If I succeed, then can I say,

With heartfelt ecstasy,

"O death! Where is they sting? O, grave!

Where is they victory?"

C. R. S. B.

Mobile City Prison, Jan. 1835[14]

Although other poems were signed *Robert*, these two had his initials. Was Charles R.S. Boyington trying to make up his mind exactly *who* he was? When he used the word *Aeolian* did that mean he was like the wind, blowing around, unsettled, unsure? Or could he have meant it to show his life was out of his control?

TWENTY-ONE
ISOLATION AND DESOLATION

February 6 and 7 were so extremely cold as far south as Calhoun County, Alabama that those days became known as "Cold Friday and Saturday." Mobile also had record temperatures; it dropped to five degrees. Reports said, "Creeks not very swift were frozen over so as to bear the weight of a horse" and "frozen sap in trees caused the bark to explode with a noise like the firing of pistols in forests."[1]

Such news didn't concern Charles who was used to New Haven's bitterly cold weather. He wouldn't be going outside. What did it matter anyhow? Even though the jail had no heat, its stench and filth were more difficult to tolerate than the discomfort of being chilly.

His upcoming fate did concern him. Scratches on the walls counted down the days. Only thirteen left. Thirteen, like the number of knots in the rope of the hangman's noose and the number of steps to the scaffold, used to illustrate how unlucky the victim was. Perhaps it also served as a threat, making vivid the destiny of horse thieves and murderers.

Horse thievery reminded him of voting, something he'd never get to do, even though the 1828 extension of suffrage to non-property owning white men applied to him. He wouldn't live to be old enough, but his conviction of stealing a horse probably disenfranchised him anyhow.

His thoughts turned to Rose and her vivid descriptions of Mardi Gras, which he wouldn't see. He compared himself to slaves. Though all of them weren't imprisoned, they weren't entirely free to join the festivities according to the law he'd read. The 1826 Section 7 City of Mobile Ordinance was titled, "An ordinance to establish a City Watch and to regulate the duties of watchmen." It specified that "No ball, dance, or assembly of people of color would be permitted within the City unless they first obtain a license from the Mayor or the Alderman, with no license granted passed [sic] 1 a.m. in the morning." Those were the legal restrictions.[2]

Rose didn't visit those last few days. She sent a note saying her father had her under his watchful eye and she couldn't slip away. She promised, no matter what, to be at the execution. Knowing how painful that would be for his love, Charles thought of replying, telling her not to come. But they'd talked about his trying to escape at the last moment, maybe with her help. Neither could give up that far-fetched hope.[3]

Reverend Hamilton made a final attempt to make Charles a believer and save his soul. To prove he held fast to his convictions, Boyington read him an unpublished poem he'd written earlier that focused upon incidents of his youth:

No. III

Fragments ...

THE MISANTHROPE.

I have beheld such scenes as would have made

A heart less callous than mine own shrink back

In horror. I have seen the ruffian's blade

Gleam in mine eye, and laugh'd at the attack:

Seen the fierce pirate, with a heart as black

As hell's own charnel house, yet stood and gaz'd

Unmoved; while the fleet ship stood on her tack,

And 'round the ocean's billows threat'ning rais'd

Their foaming crests, and the fork'd light'nings blaz'd.

Busy reflections hence!--memories avaunt!

Back to thy dark, sequester'd cell, and ne'er

Again, as now, my troubled spirit haunt

With scenes of by-gone, wretched days,--appear

No longer like some hoary, ancient seer,

Whisp'ring of scenes, now pass'd, but which have been

Dark as despair,--fitful as the ear

Of all hae heard, mayhap perused when

'Twas blazon'd forth by tell-tale, babbling pen.

I was not born as now I am; ah no—

There was a time when, free as air,

I bounded o'er the fields, or traced the flow
Of the ocean brook, casting the luring snare
Beneath its rippling waves; when from his lair,
Startled by my intrusive step, would spring
O'er the smooth glade, the fox or the timid hare,
And the young wood bird, from his silken wing,
Shake the fresh dew-drops of the smiling spring.

And was it love? May,, by this midnight lamp
I've seen the blighted lover sit and sigh,
When forth upon the verdant landscape, damp
With fallen dews, the distant orbs on high
Look not,--then, pacing to and fro, his eye
Would roll in frenzy, as he raging swore
To love, to hate, aye, to despise, yet die
A crack-brain'd fool; and then, when all was o'er,
Again he'd sigh and rave as oft before.

But I, who am not form'd like common men,
Who "gaze upon the world yet see it not,"—
I, to whom the ocean's wave, or mountain glen,
Shelter alone afford, and on whose lot
Fate's seal is set,--I love! I wot
The thought were mockery, and sooner far

Would I a fiend's affection seek than blot,

With love like mine, a maiden's hopes, for ah,

'Twixt me and man there stands a fearful bar!

Mobile, March, 1834 *AEOLIAN.*[4]

While reading it, Boyington seemed frenzied, upset, and puzzled. Taking a deep breath, he cocked his head. "Reverend Hamilton, I respect you and I am in your debt for your kind words and your interest in me. But, I hope this poem helps you understand who I am and why I act as I do. Life has not dealt me an easy hand. I struggle along, but belief in a higher being is not in my repertoire."

Hamilton nodded, slipped on his coat and put his hand on the prisoner's shoulder. "No matter, my friend, I must go, now, and take care of my flock. Your time is coming soon, so I won't be back until that day. I will stand by you until the end."

At the clanging of the cell door, Charles watched a rat scurry out of his cell behind the visitor. *Poor creature. Ah, but he is freer than I am. Perhaps he'll also live longer.* A lump filled his throat. *But my fate is not yet sealed—the Governor may still have a say. Or, with Rose's help, escape. Ah, Rosa, my dear, I long to hold you in my arms forever.* A smile crossed his face. *Lady Luck, please smile on me.*

TWENTY-TWO

LAST VISIT

At nine p.m. February 19, 1835, Reverend Hamilton headed for his last visit to Boyington before his scheduled execution the following day. On the way, a man he recognized as Br. [sic] Tardy stopped him on the corner of St. Emanuel and Dauphin Streets. Tardy was returning from a visit to the jail to see Boyington. Shaking his head, he said, "I stood outside the cell, unseen by the prisoner, and I was shocked to hear Boyington say, 'G—d d---n their souls!'"[1]

He continued, "I went inside and asked what I'd done to deserve this at his hands, and Boyington shrugged, saying he did not understand."

Tardy reported his retort to Boyington's indifference "…you should call on God whose existence you deny, to damn my soul and the soul of the minister, who kindly visits you though you deny there is a soul."

"I did not, sir, surely did I?" Boyington said. "If I did, I ask your pardon."

Taken aback, Tardy reminded Boyington that he'd soon stand before God. "I fear you are hardened beyond recovery! Hear this, my last advice, and apply for pardon to the God of mercy! Farewell!" With those words, he walked out of Boyington's cell.

The astonished Mr. Hamilton considered turning back, but he kept his promise to the prisoner, entered the heavy gates, and found

Boyington waiting for him. After being admitted by the night jailer to Boyington's cell, he told the prisoner, "…if you wish to be alone…say so frankly, and I will depart."

Boyington said he did not wish to be alone, that he'd been waiting for the minister, handing him four sheets of letter-sized paper. Ordering the jailer to bring another lighted candle, the minister read the letter.

My Dear, My Respected Friend:

I have raised my pen to address you, yet what shall I, what can I say to you? You have sat beside me in my lonely cell. I have listened to your kind, your generous counsel. You have been to me as a father, upon your bosom I have rested, and your kindness has drawn from me tears such as nothing but sympathy like yours could have called forth. What think you must be the feelings that animate my heart toward you? Do you, can you, will you believe me the savage I have been represented? I can hardly write. Oh, that you would, that you could, see the inmost recesses of my heart. But I will, yes, I will be calm.

You have solemnly asked me if I am guilty or innocent. The question itself implies a doubt; but I do not think it unkind. I have been a gay [sic, meaning carefree] *and wild youth; I have been thoughtless; I have been guilty, but not guilty of murder—not guilty of the crime with which report has charged me.*

I have not been a believer in the doctrines of Christianity, or am I now (I regret to say it, for I know it will pain you); but from my earliest youth I have held my word, when solemnity and sincerity pledged or paramount to everything. It may sound like boasting—I know it will—but intentional falsehood, and when I say upon my honor by the love I bear to her who bore me, as I value your friendship, and as I hope for the happiness of my friends and vindication of my memory, I am innocent of the murder of

Nathaniel Frost. I swear it by the most solemn oaths that I consider binding.

Were I to tell the world I am guilty, who would doubt it? Not one. But when in the most solemn manner I declare my innocence to every ear, every heart is sealed. 'Tis hard, 'Tis hard; but the day will, it must, come when I am no more in the land of the living, when my form shall have moulded in the tomb, then sooner or later, the world will believe that they have wronged me. That thought—oh, how consoling even now, when ere another day shall have passed, I shall be alike senseless of shame and approbation!

My dear sir, I must conclude. Even what letters I have written here have been done with difficulty. While I feel more than volumes could express, I can only say, I thank, I respect, I honor you. May every blessing attend you, and when you would feel and say something sad, think and speak of—

BOYINGTON[2]

His claim, *sooner or later, the world will believe that they have wronged me,*

reflected the expectations of some Mobilians. In their hearts, they felt justice had not been served and that, someday, it would be rectified.

"You're very smart, Charles, but very young. You don't know everything. Although you listen—and you learn more listening than talking—you can't seem to admit defeat. Sometimes, you have to lose to win; it's a lesson in humility." He shook his head, "Please try to consider that I'm correct and that there is a God. Save your soul."

Boyington didn't nod, move a muscle, or say a word.

Although Hamilton was impressed with the remarkable letter from a teenager in such dire conditions and inclined to believe him, he was dissuaded by Boyington's actions. He eventually concluded that this letter and all that Boyington had said and written was part of an "artful plan to excite sympathy and induce a pardon or at least a stay of execution."[3]

The minister reassured Boyington that he tried to befriend him. But his words didn't extend hope. He said he and a dozen men went to the spot of the murder that very evening. "They all condemn you; the whole community, almost without exception." He softened those harsh words by adding that Boyington's declaration of innocence made him tend to believe it was true, "…because it seems absolutely impossible that a man can be so hardened as you must be, if guilty, and especially at your age, not yet twenty." Yet, he admitted intelligent people swore there could be no doubt of his guilt. Saying he was staggered, [sic] he pleaded with his friend, "…end this painful suspense and tell me the truth, Are you guilty or are you not? Speak the truth or not at all!"[4]

Hanging his head, Boyington replied tearfully, "Sir, I thought you believed in me, but I do not blame you; yet another day will show I am innocent!" The insistence that he was guilty consumed him. If this minister of God could not be trusted to be objective even to a minute degree, neither could the church or any religion. It was a moment without hope.

After saying he'd think as favorably as possible, Hamilton placed his hand on Boyington's head. "Then, sir, cry for mercy to the Great God!" he said in an emotional tone of voice, adding, "…it is my duty to remind you you are rejecting the mercy of heaven and sealing your eternal doom. My task is done, I have only to say farewell, and then leave you until we meet at the bar of Judgment!"

The prisoner faced the wall and wept, speaking in a pitiful tone, still seeking something; he knew not what "…will you also leave me? I had hoped you would have accompanied me to the scaffold."

The minister said he'd grant Boyington's wish and stand by him to the last. He said a prayer, with one final appeal for the prisoner to pray. But Boyington said, "I cannot pray."

"Did you ever pray?" the minister asked.

"…when a child my mother taught me to repeat prayers; but since I have grown big enough to act for myself, I have never prayed," he admitted.

Reverend Hamilton shivered. "No wonder you have been left to run so far in sin. But now you give me your promise seriously that you will pray and not deceive me."

"I will, sir, indeed I will," he replied, but not before qualifying his statement by adding, "I'll try, at least."

#

On the day of the execution, Reverend Hamilton fulfilled his promise to stay with Boyington until the end. He prayed and they talked from ten a.m. until noon. The prisoner handed the minister two letters he'd written: one to his mother, the other to his brother Edwin, a respected clergyman. "Please give these to Sheriff Toulmin to mail," Boyington said.[5]

Then he pulled out another letter from his mother, and tears filled his eyes. "…stay with me to the last, and see me buried and write a full account of the last scene to my poor mother." His affection for her had not waned.[6]

He reached on a small shelf above his couch and took from it a folded letter, saying, "see that the person to whom this is addressed gets same, and the jailer also has promised it will be delivered."[7] The letter to Rose expressed his final feelings:

Rose, My Darling,

Today they will take me out to kill me, and I cannot help myself. Into my heart I feel the love of two pressing strongly who know I am innocent. It is you, Rosa, my dear, yes you whom I love most tenderly and my dearest mother back home in Litchfield. If I can only escape, we can then go to your father's home in France. There they will not harm us. I will escape! I will escape! Rosa, my dear, I want to live for you and you alone! Oh, my dear, my heart beats fast—my love for you will never die!

A friend will give this note to you for me. Be there and we will escape together. I love you tenderly—always!

City Prison, Saturday, Feb. 20, 1835.
ROBERT[8]

As if he knew what was in the letter, the minister warned his charge that he had no chance of being saved. "I solemnly believe were you reprieved under the gallows you would not leave the ground alive…popular indignation would probably follow, which most certainly prove fatal to you." He made one last plea, "…therefore once more I entreat you look at last to God for mercy!"[9]

The under-jailer entered with the jailer to remove the prisoner's fetters and dress him for execution. Boyington asked, "Is the Governor in town?"

"No," was the answer.

The word didn't kill the young man's hopes. He held on to the idea that he would somehow escape his fate.[10]

TWENTY-THREE

PROCESSION AND HANGING

Three weeks after Shrove Tuesday, on February 10 at 1:30 p.m., guards escorted Charles R.S. Boyington—dressed in a black suit and wearing a silk top hat—out of the big iron gates of Mobile Jail on St. Emanuel Street to a spot directly behind a coffin atop a cart drawn by one horse.[1] It moved at a slow pace, heading North toward Government Street.

Over a thousand people lined the streets for the public execution. All were not Mobilians; some had come from far away. They watched as the solemn procession made its way through the section of Mobile called *Buzzards' Roost* where butchers killed and dressed their beef, hogs, and muttons, attracting buzzards who ate the cast-offs of the cuttings. That day, a human, not animals, would be killed. But he'd be buried, leaving no cast-offs for the buzzards to consume.

Due to Boyington's literary prominence, and in deference to Rose and the de Fleur family, an exception was made to the custom of forcing the criminal to sit on his coffin, bare of flowers. But Boyington was allowed to walk behind it on the way to the gallows.[2] Still, he was flanked by the local militia, the Home Guards with E. March orderly officer for that company, and the City Troop, under Captain Carothers, to prevent problems. Like a festival, each group had a brass band, and the prisoner kept in step and time with the music. They escorted the procession and surrounded the scaffold to guard the execution.[3]

Occasionally, Boyington waved to people he knew as he walked along with his spiritual advisor Reverend William Hamilton on one side and his counsel, Edward Olcott, Esq., on the other.[4] Some waved back; others turned away. With no choice, Boyington marched on at a slow pace, headed for his destination—a spot in the woods not far from the Roper house where he used to meet Rose. A place with happier memories.[5]

Among the spectators was a young boy, J. Ogden Belknap, who never forgot standing on the corner of Government and Joachim Streets watching the procession. He remembered the crowd muttering things about a boy so young not living out his life. It impressed him, but he realized nobody could do anything to prevent the execution.

The mile and a half route was planned to pass the site of the murder at the Church Street Graveyard. As he strolled by that spot, Boyington didn't flinch. He stared straight ahead. The crowd also remained orderly, speaking in low tones, if they spoke at all. At one point, some disorder occurred when a man hiding in the weeds threw a brick and struck Boyington, but it barely nicked him and didn't require treatment.[6]

On Broad Street, picnickers paused long enough to glare at the prisoner.[7] If they heckled or called him names, it wasn't reported. As soon as they passed the west wall of the old graveyard, the bystanders resumed eating their lunch. Although the overall mood was somber, there were elements of entertainment.

Upon reaching the site of execution, Boyington paled as he stared at the scaffold and the gallows, his body tense and his lip quivering. A spark returned to his eyes. He saw the possibility of a way out and called his attorney, Edward Olcott, over. Knowing orders said the execution had to be completed by 4 p.m., he grabbed for any opportunity to escape his fate. "If I can succeed in delaying the execution till the appointed hour is passed," he said, "will you demand me from the sheriff?"[8]

Olcott shook his head. "It cannot be done, sir, the officers will most assuredly do their duty. If they fail to do so, the crowd assembled here will hang you."[9] Even those words did not dash Boyington's prospects. Determined to the end, he hung on to the idea that someway, somehow, he'd be rescued or escape. He could not face the fact that he would die.

Kill time. I'll read my statement, get the sympathy of the audience, and not let them stop me. If I can just make it past 4 o'clock, they'll have to let me go.

Attempts were made to dissuade him from reading any part of it, but Boyington insisted, and with a clear, firm voice, the young man stated:

My dear Friends, an innocent man will now address you. I tell you with an open heart, that I am innocent of the crime I am accused of. I will not keep you long, but I must tell you that the pain I have been suffering is unjust. I am accused, yes, but I am the man being murdered today. Emotion makes my lips tremble as I address you...[10]

Although he said he wouldn't speak long, the opposite was his intention. He went into great detail about his arrival in Mobile, giving an extensive history of his life in the Port City. He didn't get to the part about his departure from Mobile not being a sudden decision, or that he'd planned the visit to his mother and brother many months earlier.[11] After he read about ten pages of his declaration, Sheriff Toulmin ordered him to stop.[12]

Boyington ignored his command, believing if he could speak beyond the appointed hour, the execution could not legally take place. When the fatal hour was close, the sheriff asked Reverend Hamilton to persuade Boyington to desist.

"Mr. Boyington," Hamilton said, "the sheriff orders you to stop; the time is nearly expired. Descend with me and calmly submit to the last necessary arrangements."

Wide-eyed, Boyington replied, "Why can't I read the rest?"

Stepping close to the prisoner, Toulmin glared at him. "No, sir! Not another page. I am waiting for you."

Lips quivering, face pale, Boyington descended to the ground to delay proceedings. Spectators circled the scaffold with the military companies in the inner line of the circle. The prisoner insisted on talking with the "...doctor appointed to pronounce him dead." He'd given permission to this surgeon to use his body for galvanic experiments. Now, he tried to get him "to reanimate his body after execution."[13]

But the doctor told him, "I assure you it cannot be possible."

Boyington said, "...you shall not touch my body with a knife."

"Then...I do not want the body, and be assured I will not touch it."

In another effort to delay the execution, Boyington asked the doctor the easiest way to die and was told it was "for the lungs to be moderately inflated." He then approached Hamilton, watching the officers standing by with the shroud, and he asked, "Shall I wear my coat?"

Hamilton asked what it would signify, adding, "...either keep it or lay it aside...but do not delay the officers."[14]

With another delaying tactic, Boyington took off his coat and the minister laid it on the coffin. When he slowly removed his tie, the officers impatiently adjusted his death-dress on him and confined his arms. Boyington sighed heavily, became deadly pale, and the veins of his neck and temples were turgid. Eyes raised to heaven, he wriggled the arms tied behind him. "The ropes hurt my arms and wrists." On the arm of Hamilton, he ascended the scaffold, but refused to stand on the drop.

The macabre scene kept morbid onlookers reverently silent during the brief prayer by Hamilton:

Let us pray for the soul of Charles R.S. Boyington: To You, O God! I raise my eyes and voice and ask you to have mercy on the soul which is about to pass from its earthly body. We pray, O Father! to give him strength and light that his eyes and heart will open and receive Thee! Give him strength to make his peace with Thee and feel contrite deep down in his heart! We thank Thee, O Almighty Master! Amen.

Boyington took Hamilton's hand. "I thank you, sir, from the bottom of my heart."

"Boyington!" exclaimed the minister, "In a few moments you will stand before God! What is your last declaration?"

His body shaking and with eyes full of tears, Boyington kept his voice steady and clear as he loudly proclaimed with bitter words, "Sir, I am innocent! I am innocent!" he insisted. "But what can I do? When I am buried, an oak tree with a hundred roots will grow out of my grave to prove my innocence!"

Reverend Hamilton pointed toward heaven. "Look to the Lamb of God, whose blood cleanses from all sin, and cry sincerely for mercy!"

If the Reverend thought Boyington was about to repent, he was disappointed. Boyington's real aim became evident in his next remark. "…I must make an effort to save my life! May I jump from the scaffold and try to save my life?"

"No, sir,…'tis folly—'tis madness! You cannot escape. Look at all the multitude. Not a man but believes your doom richly merited. If you attempt to escape you cannot succeed, but you will be the death of some of the crowd, for the soldiers will fire!"

"No, they won't fire!" Boyington protested. "…I must make one effort for my life!"

The Reverend said he'd tried everything to save him and ended by saying, "…Farewell."

His best friend's "Farewell," caused Boyington to keep silent a few seconds, then he glanced at the crowd. On the shoulders of a man, he saw his girlfriend waving at him.[15] They made eye contact, and she mouthed the words, "I love you."

Boyington blurted out, "I must make one more effort for my life—I must!"[16] He bolted, but a deputy grabbed his arm and stopped him.

Before anything else transpired, as the minister descended the scaffold steps, a deputy adjusted the rope, Sheriff Toulmin fainted while approaching a friend, who also fainted. Oddly, the sheriff's horse "dropped in his harness the same as if he had fainted, too."[17]

Since Toulmin had been commissioned sheriff in September, it was probably the first execution he'd attended, an unnerving shock that caused his loss of consciousness. But the horse's reaction couldn't be explained.

Boyington also reacted. Taking those incidents as demonstrating sympathy, with a screech of despair, he leapt from the platform, managed to throw the rope over his head, and landed on the ground much like an agile cat.

Still tied and trembling, his knees failed him as he attempted to run. He was in the middle of the military lines. Aghast and dumbfounded, not one spectator aided or encouraged him. No one even uttered a word. Instead of gaining his freedom, he heard a command.

"Charge Bayonets!" Messengers of death approaching made him tremble. The officers seized his shaking body, forced him back up the steps, annihilating his struggle. In the struggles, the ropes loosened; his hands became free, and he scratched his captors and tore their clothes.[18] His distorted expression and wide-eyed animalistic glare showed his agony and despair.

Still, he refused to give up. When forced into the readjusted noose attached to the proper hook and thrust off his foothold, he carefully avoided struggling with his feet until the last moment of consciousness, hoping to be resuscitated. He extended his foot to try to get it back on the board he'd been pushed from and inserted his hands between the rope and his neck.

Silence prevailed among the mesmerized crowd. Officers pulled Boyington's hands away from his neck as the suspended victim swung back and forth, writhing about, attempting to prevent the inevitable. At this point, he could do nothing to avoid suffocation.

Spectators gasped. It appeared to them that the officers were weighing Boyington down to ensure speedier death and cries of horror broke out from the observers. "Oh, it is like murder!—It is murder!"[19]

The uproar of horror permeated the crowd, but soon subsided. Silence returned until half an hour later when the body of Boyington was removed and placed in his ten-dollar coffin.[20]

The crowd dispersed. Reverend Hamilton and a few people who knew Boyington went to the Old Church Street Cemetery.

The prisoner's body was buried in the northwest corner of Potter's Field near the Bayou Street wall about sixty yards from where Nathaniel Frost was murdered.[21] Head lowered, Reverend Hamilton walked away mumbling to himself, "I tried, but I failed. May God bless Charles Boyington."

A headstone, placed on Boyington's grave by friends of Nathaniel Frost, remained until 1905. It read:

Charles R. S. Boyington

Hanged for the Murder

of

NATHANIEL FROST

February 20th, 1835

The March 9, 1835, Hale Collection of Cemetery Inscriptions and Newspaper Notices of Connecticut listed Charles Boyington of Mobile and of Litchfield, Connecticut as being executed on February 20. It gave his age as twenty-one. Later a marker giving Boyington's name and the date of execution was put on the grave site. It remained until 1971. In 1985, the Forestry Commission placed a plaque on the site designating it as a Famous and Historical Tree.

Older Mobilians claimed that, before the Civil War, a woman would burn a candle at the head of the grave and place a bouquet of white flowers in a small urn at its foot on All Saints' Day.[22]

Reverend William Hamilton kept his promise to write to a friend and neighbor of Boyington's in Litchfield, CT, so his mother could hear the news gently. His letter was published in The Mobile Mercantile Advertiser on Saturday, April 11, 1835, and in other Mobile papers and other Southern newspapers, after it was first published in The Newark Daily Advertiser:

Mobile, Feb. 23, 1835

In as much as the late Charles R. S. Boyington a few hours before his execution on Friday last Feb. 20th put into my hands a letter from you as a friend delivering his mother's charge to her unhappy boy, in expectation of his speedy dismissal from earth, I know, in charge of a promise given to the poor young man communicative to his afflicted parent through you as a friend, the mournful tiding of his death according to the sentence of the law. I visited him repeatedly in his cell, sat with him there for hours; by night and by day—I warned him; I entreated him to turn to God—to repent of his sins—and trust in Christ, whose blood cleanseth from all guilt—and if guilty of the fearful crime for which he was condemned, to un bosom himself to me, or to some other person in whom he might have confidence. I solemnly promised him that if he should wish to confide anything to me, either a confession of his guilt or anything else, it should be sacredly locked up in my bosom till the judgment day, unless he should authorize me to divulge it. He solemnly asserted his innocence, and I did believe him; I felt for him as a poor child; I wept for him and we wept together. On Thursday night he put into my hands a letter very affectionately addressed to me, and still asserting his innocence of the crime of murder. He was, I presume you know, entirely skeptical on the subject of religion; he not only rejected the Gospel and denied the immorality of the soul, but he denied the existence of God. After some interview with him, he admitted the being of a God and seemed wavering as to the soul's immortality; but on every other point he remained unchanged in sentiment. On Friday morning I again went to his cell about 10 o'clock, and continued with him until about half past 12, when the deputy sheriff came to knock off his chains and prepare him for the last awful scene. At his request the night before I had promised to accompany him to the scaffold, be with him to the last, and see his body covered in the grass. He walked between me and his counsel, a most amiable man, from the jail to the scaffold about two and a half miles. All this time he had maintained an appearance of firmness. I had forewarned him that escape, resistance, pardon and reprieve were all alike helpless. I promised him that in the last moment I would stand by his side—and pray for him, and that to the last I would watch his eye, and be ready to hear should he relent or wish to speak—to confess—or to breathe or cry for mercy; that done, I entreated him to be firm and self-possessed in his last moment.

Alas! It pains me to say his conduct at last showed clearly he had never in all these trying scenes fully believed he must die; he certainly was buoying up his spirits with the hope of escape, either by passing the hour fixed for his execution or by a reprieve—or by exciting the sympathy of the bystanders; to attempt a rescue. This is a very painful subject, but I pledged my word to write to his friends a full statement of the case. After he had read from a defence [sic] he had prepared till the sheriff announced the time when stop he must—I ascended the scaffold with him and his last arrangements were made; I led him once more, he holding my arm up the steps—there I once more prayed by him commending him to the mercy of God—the vast multitude maintaining a profound silence; when done, he took my hand—thanked me for my kindness with exceeding agitation, and asked, 'what must I do?' Thinking he was relenting, I pointed to heaven, saying 'look even now to the Lamb of God and cry for mercy!' I asked what is your last declaration, for in a few moments you will be in eternity? He answered—'I am innocent, but may I not try to escape?' I pointed out the impossibility, the madness of the attempt, told him if he tried, the Guards would fire and some in the crowd would be killed. He said 'oh, no! they won't, I must try.' Boyington, (I said) I have done—I have tried to be faithful to your soul and now farewell!—'You have been faithful' was his answer, 'but I must make an effort for my life, I must,' and as I turned to descend, he sprang from the scaffold, and in a few moments all was over! Oh, that awful—that terrible scene! For several nights I had scarcely any sleep—that night was a night of horrors and agony to me at the remembrance of what I had witnessed! I waited, accompanied the body to the grave, and saw it decently interred. Break this dreadful intelligence as gently as you can to the poor mother, hardened and unchanged to the last the poor youth was. Till the last hope of escape or rescue was gone he remained unmoved; and then, with an expression of agony such as I have never before beheld, he made his fruitless spring for life.

O tell the poor, desolate mother she must look to God for support, I can offer her no consolation except what springs from a consideration of the rectitude of His Government; to His kind support I devoutly commend her. My own feelings have been too deeply wounded on this trying occasion to attempt offering consolation to others. My task is now ended—poorly performed but not without emotion of sympathy for pain I might inflict—Farewell!

WM. T. HAMILTON[23]

Were Hamilton's words "I did believe him" the whole truth? Or did he simply want to soften the blows of the gruesome tale and give some comfort to the teenager's mother? Could they have been written by this minister, a true believer, to try to convince himself that no young person could be so much in denial of God? Only God

TWENTY-FOUR

THEORIES, UNSOLVED MYSTERY, CLOSING THE BOOK

Years later, on All Saints' Day, Rose slipped out of her house at six a.m. But she didn't go to church. Walking at a fast clip in sprinkles of rain, she headed for the site of her fiancé's execution, wishing she'd brought her parasol.

Memories flooded her mind: Strolling along to that same spot with Charles Robert, her beloved, at her side, the beauty of the unspoiled flower and fauna, the peacefulness with only the birds singing to them, Robert sneaking a kiss when Lydia wasn't looking.

As she neared Bayou Street, a milkman pulled his horse to a stop. "Are you all right, Miss?" he asked. "You'll catch your death of cold in this weather."

Rose nodded. "Yes, I'm fine." She lifted her skirt and stepped across a puddle of water from the heavy rain of the night before. "I'm not going far, just a few blocks." The man's horse reminded her of the one carrying Charles' coffin on this same street and she blurted out, "and then I'm coming back to the graveyard."

"I see." He shook his head and pointed down Bayou Street to the site of Charles' grave. "I ain't been near that graveyard since that hanging. Whooee! That brought some folks to town. It ain't forgotten, neither. People talk about it all the time. Big old oak grew there like the murderer said it would, didn't it? Those two fellows will be remembered forever by that location. But I don't recall their names, do you?" He didn't wait for a reply. "I jes' know they became permanent residents sooner than they expected." He guffawed. "They's both buried there, ain't they?"

Staring back at him, Rose sucked in her breath and tightened the scarf around her neck.

"Oh, I didn't mean to bring up nothing to upset you, Miss. You be careful now, y'hear? I gotta be going." The milkman slapped the rein on the horse's hind quarter, prodding the animal to trot forward.

Minutes later, Rose arrived at her destination. This time, a crew of men hammering the finishing touches on the Roper home broke the peace. The magnificence if the Greek Revival house made her gasp. Other workers were busy, too. The surrounding area was full of landscapers, some sodding the front lawn; others adding azaleas to shrub beds. The scent of fresh grass and overturned dirt filled the air.

Rose stopped in her tracks and glanced first in one direction, then in another. Some of the trees and brush of the thirty-three acres had been cleared, so she couldn't pinpoint the exact spot of the hanging, but she saw one large oak she thought she'd stood by awaiting a chance to escape with her lover. In her mind's eye, Rose envisioned the scaffold. She blinked, shuddering at the memory. Then she mouthed the words of the Lord's Prayer, ending with "God bless you, Robert, wherever you are."

A workman touched his coworker's shoulder and pointed to her. Not wanting to make any excuses for being there, Rose scurried away before they could approach.

Her next stop was at the Church Street Graveyard. Although the marker for Robert's gravesite had disappeared, finding the spot of his burial was easy. Rose went straight to it and, without a thought of ruining her dress, plopped down onto wet grass beside the live oak that grew on the site, just as Robert had predicted it would to prove his innocence.

Rose shoved a damp curl off her forehead and pulled a piece of paper folded in a square to form an envelope out of her pocket. She read the words of the poems he'd written to her on the best hand-made writing paper of the 1830s. It was one she'd treasured and reread time after time:

TO ROSE

I saw a lovely butterfly

Light on the bosom of a winter rose;

He kissed the stamens one by one,

Then flew away as in a love-sick pose.

A tear trickled down her cheek as she bemoaned the fact that they didn't fly away. She scanned the next two verses before reading the fourth one aloud.

The raindrops beat down the rose

Until it hung low its lovely head,

And when I returned next eve

I found, too, the butterfly was dead.

The symbolism was clear, and the words rang true, too true. Rosa read on:

So if I had been the butterflyAnd you the lovely winter rose,

I would do the same, methinks,

And call down the blinding snows!

True love is the greatest thing

In life a man can own;

Oh, 'tis you, my lovely, Rose,

I love and you alone[1]

And her love for Boyington went unrequited. But why? Did that really have to happen? Or should they have been together forever?

The rain had stopped, but Rose's face remained wet with tears. Her face sank into cupped hands. "Robert, my dear Robert. Was justice done? You said sooner or later you'd be vindicated." She took a deep breath. "But you haven't."

Rose raised her eyes to the heavens. "What is the truth? Did you do it, Charles?" Plucking a leaf from the eight-foot-tall oak tree, she stared at it. "I know this tells me you didn't, and I want to believe it, but you had the motive, the opportunity and the method—your knife."

"I also know Papa would have done almost anything to keep me away from you. He didn't want me to marry below my class, especially to someone who wasn't Catholic; worse yet, someone who professed no religion." She sighed. *And how did Papa wind up? After a confrontation with a French count, he left Mama and me and returned to France.*[2] *I don't know the details of that event, but I do know Papa had a duel in France and his victim succumbed. So, I have to acknowledge that he wasn't above committing murder. All this was shortly after you were...Oh, I can't say it, even now."*

She covered her mouth with both hands. "I don't think I believe Florence White, the prostitute who confessed to the crime; she could have just wanted attention. And I can't believe my own father would do this and allow my beloved to be executed for the crime. No, I won't accept that."

Letting her hands drop to her lap, she took a deep breath and stiffened her shoulders. "And Captain George confessed to the crime on his deathbed. They said he produced Frost's Lepine watch to prove he was the murderer.[3] But what was his motive? Why can't I simply believe his statement and accept it? Why doesn't anybody think he told the truth? Is it too pat? Nobody's willing to take his word and reopen the investigation, so maybe it is. Why would he confess to a crime he didn't commit?" She chewed on the corner of her lip, drew blood and wiped it away with her handkerchief. "If he did kill Nathaniel, did it have something to do with Charles's gambling debts? But what?"

She gazed into space. "Maybe I'm wrong about that woman. Robert told the police another passenger on the Cahaba said she was *using* Frost. But Nathaniel denied it. He gave Robert his wallet in the cemetery to prove he had money and that she wasn't using him. Oh, Robert, you claimed she did kill Frost."[4]

She squinted. "On second thought, maybe Florence White was Captain George's paramour. Reports circulated that she and a male companion lured Frost to the cemetery to rob him. The captain could have been the 'companion' with her when the murder was committed. Maybe they needed money to run away together." The idea rattled around in her brain, and she concluded, "No, They said that man died with delirium tremens. Besides, that's too far-fetched."

Rose mulled over the facts of the case as she speculated on different people's motives. *If Captain George thought Frost wasn't going to give Robert the money to pay his gambling debts, maybe he went into a rage, and it ended in murder. If Papa did it, his motive was clear; he was preventing our marriage.* She stared at the oak that seemed to be growing in front of her eyes. *If you did it, Charles, then why did this tree grow?* She looked to her left and right, casting her eyes on four other live oaks within a few yards.

Lots of acorns fall here, but this one is directly over your grave. Is it testifying to your innocence? At least your trial did some good; it changed the way grand juries were selected, ensuring that non-citizens can't serve. Maybe lawyers will stop people already convinced of guilt or innocence from serving, too.

Rose stood and shook her head. The clouds cleared enough for the early morning sun to peek through. She reached out and touched a high branch of the oak. "You've grown, and it's time for me to do the same. I'm still young; I need to move on, to continue my life. Goodbye, Charles Robert Boyington."

Charles's pet name for her echoed in her ears. "Goodbye, Rosa, my dear."

Rose faced the one undeniable fact: Charles was the last person seen walking with Nathaniel the afternoon of the murder. Still, it's only circumstantial evidence, the type the entire case had hinged on. *Maybe someone with him wasn't seen. In any event, it's highly unlikely anybody will ever know the truth about who killed Nathaniel Frost.*

She removed the gold chain with the heart Charles had carved for her and slipped it onto a low branch of the tree, behind leaves and out of sight of passersby. With her posture as straight as his once was, finding her way around puddles, she took long strides toward her future, and never looked back.

AFTERWORD

It's a curiosity that Boyington expected to be acquitted, until it's considered that several murders had been committed since he arrived in Mobile, but no man had been convicted.[1]

Later events that developed were also odd. It sometimes happens that people confess to crimes they did not commit. This could have occurred in the Boyington case. It was odd that two people admitted to the crime 48 years apart. One was a man, the other a woman.

In the summer of 1847, when he was dying, Captain William George confessed to murdering his tenant.[2] Speculation had it that George stole Frost's money, and when the printer accused him of the theft, he retaliated by killing his boarder.

A woman named Florence White claimed she killed Frost. The admission was made on her deathbed, sixty years after the crime. Rumors suggested she was a prostitute who simply wanted attention, a way to avert being remembered as immoral and become immortal, distorted as the concept may be.[3] Whether either confession had any validity remains unknown.

A newspaper article entitled *The Wrong Man Hung* in the Albany Evening Journal, August 23, 1847, touted his innocence. It said:

A young printer named Boyington, who served his time in the office of the New Haven Palladium, was hung a few years since in Alabama, upon a charge of having murdered a companion with whom he was traveling. He protested his innocence to the last, but without avail. Recently the landlord, in whose house the murder was committed [sic], confessed the crime on his death-bed! Boyington was a young man of fine talents and preposing [sic] appearance, whose guilt was deemed conclusive only from the fact that he was the last person seen with the murdered man.[4]

Although the writer misidentified the location of the murder, he seemed firm in his conviction.

Other sources claimed Charles had serious problems in his youth. They said the horse theft wasn't his only crime and reported that he'd committed felonies and piracy. Reports were that he was suspected of multiple thefts in Boston, had been arrested at Savannah and was supposedly convicted of piracy there. Luckily, his extreme youth got him a pardon for that offense.[5]

All those wrongdoings took place as Boyington made his journey from New England to Mobile working at stops on the way as an itinerant journeyman printer. Charles vehemently denied the piracy charge, one that William Hamilton said he considered "unfounded."[6]

But Charles reputation wasn't favorable even in his youth. One sea captain who knew him as a schoolboy said he lacked self-control and was dishonest and restless even in those days of his early childhood. Charles insisted all of that was a mistake.

A better reputation may have caused less suspicion regarding Frost's murder, but as William Hamilton noted, a bad name helped send him to the gallows.[7]

The minister saw some good come from that execution. He thought young people, like Boyington, commit crimes hoping for impunity. He felt the Boyington story could set an example. He cautioned youngsters to "Beware then of the beginning of folly! Beware of the first step in guilt! Beware!" He intended to warn teenagers that "PUNISHMENT will overtake the evil-doer in the end!"[8]

Older Mobilians such as Mrs. Sarah DeBois, respected as the First Matron of the City Hospital of Mobile, and J. Ogden Belknap also spoke of unfavorable opinions of Boyington. They claimed he was known as "somewhat of a sham, pretending to be one thing yet was another." They claimed he refused jobs and hung out in bar rooms and brothels in Spanish Alley near the riverfront. Plus, that, they felt his skepticism "went against him" in the trial. The vices of his youth sullied his name.[9]

Guilty or innocent, even though dead, the name Boyington did not stay out of court. In June 1837, Zachariah Middleton, like Boyington, challenged the qualifications of a grand juror to quash an indictment when the Supreme Court considered the case. A rising young attorney named Elisha Wolsey Peck faced the court headed by future Governor Henry W. Collier. This was an entirely different court from Boyington's, and it wasted no time overturning the precedent set by the Boyington case, stating, "the forms which the law has prescribed, as preparatory to its punishment, should be observed." Grand jurors had to be properly qualified.[10]

The Boyington case had a far-reaching influence. Sixty years after Boyington's was hanged, in September, 1894, while summing up before a jury in Judge John Tyson's court in Hayneville, Alabama, the Honorable J.C. Richardson illustrated how strong circumstantial evidence may be mistaken, using the Boyington case as an example.

He said that a number of years after Boyington was hanged, Florence White summoned Mobile's chief of police as she was dying. She told him her conscience had "almost driven her crazy." Then she produced a watch with a chain and a fob and a diamond ring, explain how "her man" followed Frost and Boyington hoping to rob them. He had overheard the two men plan to go to the cemetery, and he persuaded Florence to go with him because Frost liked her. Since Frost was very drunk at the time, they'd be able to take his money.

When Boyington left, Florence and the man came out of hiding and surprised Frost. She said she intended to rob him while he slept, but he was awake, and he refused to comply with their orders, even after the man hit him with a club. Wanting his money, Florence took the knife Boyington had given Frost away from him and "plunged it into his heart time after time." Then the two dragged the body over the wall and hid it in the bushes.

Florence said "her man" took the money, had a spree, and died with delirium tremens. Not long after this Florence died. The police chief "made a solemn oath never again to recommend conviction of a person purely on circumstantial evidence."[11]

White's statement had a huge impact. *True Detective Mysteries* reported that *The entire State of Alabama, as well as the rest of the country, was so shocked by the terrible tragedy Florence White's confession revealed that it brought a change in the criminal jurisprudence not only in Alabama, but also many other states. After that it was almost impossible to get a conviction solely on circumstantial evidence."*[12]

Many *What if's* surfaced about this case. What if Boyington had been tried after Collier's ruling regarding jury choices? What if Boyington's jury had decided circumstantial evidence alone was not adequate for a conviction? What if George or White had come forward during the trial?

Answers to all the *what if's* in the world can't change the results of the Boyington case. He won't be resurrected from the dead after almost two centuries. Yet young men wrote notes in their girlfriends' autograph books referring to Boyington long after he died, up until after the Civil War. People still visit his gravesite, and some claim they hear cries of the teenager as they stand next to the enormous oak fulfilling his prediction that it would have a hundred roots and testify to his innocence.

Since no one has provided any new evidence, it is highly unlikely that Boyington's innocence will be proclaimed and his name will be cleared. Nonetheless, he hasn't been forgotten. In 2019, Haint Blue Brewing Company—located in the old, iconic Crystal Ice House, which backs up to the Church Street Graveyard—named a beer *Berried Truth* (Berliner Weisse)[13] in Boyington's honor. It is highly likely that the name Charles R.S. Boyington will long remain in the annals of history.

AUTHOR'S FINAL NOTES

Charles Robert S. Boyington, who were you, a murderer, or a misunderstood soul? You had a deceptive side; you pretended to be 23 years old but admitted in a letter that you had not reached your 20th year. But did that deception extend to other areas of your life?

Were you carrying out plans to visit your family in New Haven, CT when you left Mobile or running to escape a charge of murder?

You had the expertise to be a printer, but hard work was not your forte. Perhaps that's because you'd rather write eloquent poetry and exercise your masterful ability to make words come to life. Where did you get such talent without formal higher education? Were you of superior intellect and self-educated? Also, you had musical talent. Who taught you to play the harp, the mandolin, and the lute?

As an atheist, what inspired you? You always seemed to have a goal, perhaps to accumulate wealth. But you didn't force yourself to pursue it. In fact, by not being conscientious on the job, you lost it. That's a contradiction in behavior.

Did you fall in love at first sight with Rose, or was it an ambitious ploy to be accepted into Mobile society? Perhaps at first, you planned to use Rose, but later it turned into true love reflected in the poetry you wrote for her while in jail.

Your strong feelings for nature and your references to God in your poetry and in a letter to your mother suggest you may have worn a mask. Could that have been to project an image of a man of the world? Claiming to be 23 suggests you felt a need to deny being a believer in a superior being to avoid being patronized as an immature teenager. You did take great pride in being a card sharp. And you did not show a clear understanding of distinguishing ego and self-confidence. For you, they seemed to overlap.

Maybe sheer confidence in yourself as the be-all, end-all, was based on your youth, your optimism, and your ability to escape. Plus you had charm, unequaled power of persuasion, and the gift of using language to present your best self.

No doubt, you were a survivor who hung on to hope. You thought you'd never be convicted of murder, or if you were, you expected the governor to intervene, even during your last hours. At your hanging, you made a desperate last effort to escape. Perhaps you thought you could bend reality to fit your will as you had often done in your short life.

Your eloquent final statement showed you never gave up. More impacting, you did not give up when referring to the afterlife, although you claimed not to believe in it. You boldly stated that an oak would grow on your gravesite to prove your innocence. Your prediction came true.

Ah, the tragedy of it all. Who knows what might have been? You and Rose could have had a future together. Your children may have inherited your intelligence and creative ability, and they could have become famous in their own right. You moved people with your poetry. You had a following even while in prison. Your talent could have positively influenced your community. But you died, and it was denied.

Was justice served, or did you deserve your fate? Only you and the victim know, and neither can reveal the truth of the matter.

Charles Robert S. Boyington you can only be classified as an enigma!

ACKNOWLEDGMENTS

Many thanks to Maureen Maclay who sparked my interest in this topic, even though she decided not to join forces in writing the book. She wrote the appealing Foreword, contributed the chapter on Patsey with its excellent imagery, and provided research material, all of which added flavor to the story. And she was a Beta reader with precise attention to content.

I offer my gratitude to Shannon Brown, who set up meetings with knowledgeable people, went on interviews, and helped me research. She did a marvelous job of editing the book and making sure the format was correct.

Margaret Powers also went with me on interviews and helped copy news clips and other pertinent material.

Ben Davis cast his perceptive eye on the manuscript and suggested changes that made the writing flow smoothly. His noteworthy comment about the book was, "I think you've even raised the romantic in this old codger."

Beth Armfield said she could "find dead people," and she did. The copies of that research she made for me enhanced this book. Her tireless effort to dig a little deeper and unearth pertinent facts are greatly appreciated.

The enthusiastic support of John Tyson, former Mobile District Attorney, is much appreciated, especially his input about his great-grandfather John Tyson who presided over a case in 1894 in Hayneville, Alabama. In that case, another judge mentioned Boyington as proof that mistakes can be made regarding circumstantial evidence. That led to convictions solely on circumstantial evidence becoming very difficult to obtain, not only in Alabama, but also in other states.

Thanks to my children—Harry for technical advice; Denis for the cover design; Mike for taking photos; and Marcia for input regarding content. Thanks to my brother Jack Schluter for guidance regarding the rules of the game of poker.

My gratitude goes out to Rachel Fenske, who spent hours helping me find pertinent information and making copies to ensure it was recorded accurately.

Thanks also to Dr. Bernard Eichold for valuable information about infectious diseases, such as tuberculosis, Tighe Marston, who provided information about Boyington's burial spot, Marie Solomon who supplied many details about the former old City Jail, and to Paula Webb who suggested places to research.

I am grateful to my Beta readers who diligently checked the manuscript searching for errors. This includes Cassandra King, Margaret Daniels, Ken Wall, Dr. Ned Swanner, and Maureen Maclay. Their time and efforts were invaluable.

Others whose contributions were very helpful are Charles Torrey and Seth Kinard who resurrected files from long ago as did Mike Avery, Edward Harkins, Tamara Collier, Pamela Major, and Nancy Dupree. John Sledge also provided useful information and encouragement.

Without the dedicated assistance of all of these people, this rendition of Charles R. S. Boyington's story may never have been told.

ENDNOTES

Introduction

[1]Diard, p. 101

CHAPTER ONE

[1]Diard, p. 56

[2]Gulf Coast Review, p. 17

[3]Diard, p. 59

[4]Diard, p. 9

[5]Diard, p. 3

[6]Gulf Coast Historical Review, p. 10

[7]Diard, p. 88

[8]Diard, p. 88

[9]www.poets. org

[10]Diard, p. 65

[11]Diard, p. 66

[12]Diard, p.87

[13]Diard, p. 86-88

[14]Diard, p. 92

[15]Diard, p. 93

[16]Diard, p. 85

[17]Diard, p. 91-92

[18]Diard, p. 65

CHAPTER TWO

[1]www.encyclopediaofalabama.org/Padgett

[2]Diard, p. 53, 63

[3]Inge, Herndon, Historic Mobile Preservation Society, Interview, April 02, 2019

[4]Inge, Herndon, Historic Mobile Preservation Society, Interview, April 02, 2019

CHAPTER THREE

[1]www.genealogy.com

[2]www.genealogy.com

[3]www.genealogy.com

[4]www.genoalogy.com

[5]Eichold, MD, Bernard, Interview, January 22, 2019

[6]Diard, p. 89-9

CHAPTER FOUR

[1]Blaufaub, Rafe

[2]Diard, p. 91-92

CHAPTER FIVE – NONE

CHAPTER SIX

[1]Mercantile Advertiser, 1835, Boyington Statement, p. 32

CHAPTER SEVEN

[1]Kirby, Brendan, Mobile Press-Register, 200th Anniversary, June 19. 2013

CHAPTER EIGHT

[1]www.genealogy.com

[2]www.encyclopediaalabama.com

CHAPTER NINE

[1]Diard, p. 6

[2]Diard, p. 100

[3]Diard, p. 103

CHAPTER TEN – NONE

CHAPTER – ELEVEN

[1]Mercantile Advertiser, 1835, Boyington Statement, p. 5

[2]Mercantile Advertiser, 1835, Boyington Statement, p. 5

[3]Mercantile Advertiser, 1835, Boyington Statement, p. 32

[4]Diard, p. 66-67

CHAPTER TWELVE – NONE

CHAPTER THIRTEEN

[1]Mercantile Advertiser, 1835, Boyington Statement, p. 7

[2]Mercantile Advertiser, 1835, Boyington Statement, p. 7

[3]Mercantile Advertiser, 1835, Boyington Statement, p. 7

[4]Mercantile Advertiser, 1835, Boyington Statement, p. 6

[5]Diard, p. 102

[6]Mercantile Advertiser, 1835, Boyington Statement, p. 11

CHAPTER FOURTEEN

[1]Johnson, Alvin, Craighead, p. 32

[2]Case in 2nd Porter Supreme Court Reports, p. 100

[3]http://montomom.tripod.com/Boyington Oak

[4]Landmark Hall, 09 August, 1879, p. 102

[5]Landmark Hall, 09 August, 1879, p. 102

CHAPTER FIFTEEN

[1]Mobile Daily Register, 1879

[2]Mercantile Advertiser, May 19, 1834

[3]Diard, p. 4

[4]Diard, p. 4

[5]Diard, p. 5

[6]Diard, p. 5

[7]Diard, p. 5

[8]Mobile Commercial Register and Patriot, Monday, May 12, 1834, p. 02, Col. 5, Diard, p. 2

[9]Diard, p. 4

[10]Diard, p. 5

[11]Diard, p. 6

[12]Diard, p. 7

[13]Mobile Commercial Register and Patriot, Wednesday May 14, 1834, p. 01, Col. 5

[14]Mobile Commercial Register and Patriot, Thursday Evening, May 15, 1834, p. 2, Col. 1

[15]Diard, p. 6

[16]Mobile Commercial Register and Patriot, May 18, 1834, p. 2, Col. 1

[17]Mobile Commercial Register and Patriot, May 19, 1834, p. 2, Col. 1

[18]Mobile Mercantile Advertiser, May 19, 1834, p. 42

[19]Mobile Mercantile Advertiser, May 19, 1834, p. 42

[20]Solomon Interview, April 02, 2019

[21]Mobile Sunday Register, July 26, 1931

[22]Diard, p. 7

[23]Diard, p. 7-8

CHAPTER SIXTEEN

[1]Mobile Mercantile Advertiser, 1835, Boyington Statement, p. 4

[2]Mobile Mercantile Advertiser, 1835, Boyington Statement, p. 4

[3]Mobile Mercantile Advertiser, 1835, Boyington Statement, p. 5

[4]Mobile Mercantile Advertiser, 1835, Boyington Statement, p. 6

[5]Mobile Mercantile Advertiser, 1835, Boyington Statement, p. 6

[6]Mobile Mercantile Advertiser, 1835, Boyington Statement, p. 17

[7]Mobile Mercantile Advertiser, 1835, Boyington Statement, p. 18

[8]Mobile Mercantile Advertiser, 1835, Boyington Statement, p. 18

CHAPTER SEVENTEEN

[1]Diard, p. 41

[2]Diard, p. 68

[3]Mobile Mercantile Advertiser, April, 1834

[4]Diard, p. 69

[5]Diard, p. 7

[6]Diard, p. 69-70

[7]Diard, p. 13

[8]Diard, p. 13

[9]Diard, p. 13

[10]Diard, p. 13

[11]Diard, p. 13

CHAPTER EIGHTEEN

[1]Diard, p. 9

[2]Diard, p. 8

[3]Mobile Mercantile Advertiser, Vol. 01, No. 180, p. 02, Col. 01, May 17, 1834

[4]Diard, p. 14-15

[5]Diard, p. 15

[6]Diard, p. 19

[7]Diard, p. 18

[8]Diard, p. 19

[9]Diard, p. 19

[10]Diard, p. 20-21

[11]Diard, p. 24

CHAPTER NINETEEN

[1]Diard, p. 9

[2]Diard, p. 9

[3]Garrett, p. 44

[4]Diard, p. 9

[5]Diard, p. 10

[6]Diard, p. 12

[7]Diard, p. 12

[8]Diard, p. 10

[9]Garrett, p. 44

[10]Diard, p. 9

[11]Craighead, p. 36

[12]Courthouse Mobile County, Vol. 1833-1836 period, p. 229

[13]Diard, p. 10

[14]Supreme Court 100, 2nd Port. 100, Supreme Court of Alabama, 7 Coke 18

[15]Supreme Court 124

[15]Supreme Court 8

[17]Supreme Court 8

[18]Supreme Court 15, 16

[19]Gulf Coast Historical Review, p. 29

[20]Craighead, p. 33

[21]Craighead, p. 36

[22]Mobile Mercantile Advertiser, 1835, Boyington Statement, p. 4

[23]Mobile Mercantile Advertiser, 1835, Boyington Statement, p. 5

[24]Mobile Mercantile Advertiser, 1835, Boyington Statement, p. 7

[25]Gulf Coast Historical Review, p. 12

[26]Mobile Mercantile Advertiser, 1835, Boyington Statement, p. 14

[27]Mobile Mercantile Advertiser, 1835. Boyington Statement, p. 14

[28]Mobile Mercantile Advertiser, 1835, Boyington Statement, p. 15

[29]Mobile Mercantile Advertiser, 1835, Boyington Statement, p. 17

[30]Mobile Mercantile Advertiser, 1835, Boyington Statement, p. 19

[31]Mobile Mercantile Advertiser, 1835, Boyington Statement, p. 19

[32]Mobile Mercantile Advertiser, 1835, Boyington Statement, p. 19

[33]Mobile Mercantile Advertiser, 1835, Boyington Statement, p. 20

[34]Mobile Mercantile Advertiser, 1835, Boyington Statement, p. 21

[35]Salem Register, Vol. XLVIII, P. 02

CHAPTER TWENTY

[1]Diard, p. 63

[2]Diard, p. 64

[3]Craighead, p. 35

[4]Diard, p. 65

[5]Mobile Mercantile Advertiser, 1835, Boyington Statement, p. 22

[6]Mobile Mercantile Advertiser, 1835, Boyington Statement, p. 22

[7]Mobile Mercantile Advertiser, 1835, Boyington Statement, p. 27

[8]Mobile Mercantile Advertiser, 1835, Boyington Statement, p. 27

[9]Mobile Mercantile Advertiser, 1835, Boyington Statement, p. 29

[10]Mobile Mercantile Advertiser, 1835, Boyington Statement, p. 30

[11]Mobile Mercantile Advertiser, 1835, Boyington Statement, p. 30, 31

[12]Mobile Mercantile Advertiser, 1835, Boyington Statement, p. 31

[13]Mobile Mercantile Advertiser, 1835, Boyington Statement, p. 31

[14]Mobile Mercantile Advertiser, 1835, Boyington Statement, p. 38

CHAPTER TWENTY-ONE

[1]www.genealogytrails.com

[2]Ordinance, Section 07

[3]Diard, p. 103

[4]Mobile Mercantile Advertiser, p. 33

CHAPTER TWENTY-TWO

Diard, p. 25

[2]Diard, p. 27

[3]Craighead, p. 35

[4]Diard, p. 28

[5]Diard, p. 30

[6]Diard, p. 30

[7]Diard, p. 30

[8]Diard, p. 103

[9]Diard, p. 30-31

[10]Diard, p. 31

CHAPTER TWENTY-THREE

[1]Diard, p. 32

[2]Craigheard, p 32

[3]Diard, p. 33

[4]Diard, p. 32, Craighead, p. 36

[5]Craighead, p. 36

[6]Lambert Hall, Clipping Collection

[7]Diard, p. 36

[8]Diard, p. 33

[9]Craighead, p. 37

[10]Diard, p. 33 (from Mrs. Sarah DeBois' Scrapbooks)

[11]Mobile Mercantile Advertiser, 1835, Boyington Statement, p. 1-10

[12]Diard, p. 34

[13]Diard, p. 34

[14]Diard, p. 35

[15]Diard, p. 50

[16]Diard, p. 37

[17]Diard, p. 37

[18]Diard, p. 38

[19]Diard, p. 38

[20]Galloway File, 28, p. 5

[21]Diard, p. 39

[22]Diard, p. 40 (from Mrs. Sarah DeBois' Scrapbooks)

[23]Nework Daily Advertiser, Hamilton Letter

CHAPTER TWENTY-FOUR

[1]Diard, p. 66

[2]Diard, p. 41-42 (from Mrs. Sarah DeBois' Scrapbooks)

[3]Porter, 65

[4]Porter, 64-65

AFTERWORD

[1]Diard, p. 69

[2]Diard, p. 58

[3]Johnson, Alvin, Albany Evening Journal

[4]Albany Evening Journal

[5]Diard, p. 56-57

[6]Diard, p. 57

[7]Diard, p. 55

[8]Diard, p. 57

[9]Diard, p. 55

[10]Diard, p. 56

[11]Mobile Item, p. 42

[12]Mobile, Item p. 42

[13]Haint Blue Brewing Company

CENTER - POEMS

[1]Diard, p. 72, 73

[2]Diard, p. 73

[3]Diard, p. 73

[4]Diard, p. 74

[5] Diard p. 75, 76

[6]Diard, p. 77

[7]Diard, p. 77

[8]Diard, p. 77

[9]Diard, p. 77. 78

[10]Diard, p. 78

[11]Diard, p. 79

[12]Diard, p. 79

[13]Diard, p. 79

[14]Diard, p. 79

[15]Diard, p. 79

[16]Diard, p. 80

[17]Diard, p. 80

[18]Diard, p. 81-83

[19]Diard, p. 83

BIBLIOGRAPHY

Books

Craighead, Erwin, The Powers Printing Company *From Mobile's Past,* Mobile, 1925

Diard, Francois Ludgere, Gill Printing and Stationery Company, *The Tree: Being the Strange Case of Charles R. S. Boyington,* Mobile, 1949

Gulf Coast Historical Review, *Down the Years Articles on Mobile's History,* Michael Thomason, Editor, 2001

Hamilton, William T., *The Last Hours of Charles R.S. Boyington, Who Was Executed at Mobile, Alabama for the Murder of Nathaniel Frost* Mobile: (Printed at the Commercial Register Office, 1835)

History of the Church Street Graveyard

Porter, Benjamin F., *Reminiscences of Men and Things in Alabama:* Sara Walls; A Portals Book; Sara Walls; Tuscaloosa, 1983; P. 64, 65

Court Records

Boyington v. State, 2 Port. 100, Supreme Court of Alabama, January Term, 1835

Circuit Court Minutes, Book #9, 1833-1836

Porter Vol. 2, 1836

Probate Court Files 28, pgs. 2, 5, 28

2nd Porter Supreme Court Reports, p. 100

Interviews

Eichold, Dr. Bert, Personal Interview January 22,

Inge, Herndon, III, Attorney, Mobile Historical Preservation Society, Telephone and email Interviews, April 2 and April 10, 2019

King, Cassandra, Author, Telephone Interview, April 27, 2019

Solomon, Marie, Docent at Conde-Charlotte House, Personal Interview, April 9, 2019

Swanner, Dr, Ned, Attorney, Personal Interview, April 25, 2019

Wall, Ken, Attorney, Telephone Interview, May 2, 2019

Letters

E.S. Garrett, Letter to Erwin Craighead, February 9, 1933

Newspaper Articles

Albany Evening Journal, Pruitt & Higgins, *The Wrong Man Hung,* Albany, NY, August 23, 1847

Johnson, Alvin, Albany Evening Journal, *Tree Grows Through Grave 'Proving' Innocence of Man Hanged Long Ago in Mobile,* Circa 1894

Mobile Advertiser Weekly, For the Country, 8 September 1847 (Private collection of Mrs. Carter Smith)

Mobile Daily Register, *The Murder of Nathaniel Frost-Remembrances of Mobile,* Mobile, 1871

Mobile Mercantile Advertiser, May 19, 1835

Mobile Mercantile Advertiser, *Shocking Murder,* Vol. 1, No. 175, Pg. 2, Col 1, 12 May 1834

Mobile Mercantile Advertiser, May 29, 1834

Salem Register, Vol XLVIII, No. 70, p. 2, col. 7, Salem, Mass., 2 September 1847 (From Newberryport Herald letter of Boyington a few days after the trial)

Smith, Bill, Press Register, Staff Writer, *Case of Charles Boyington Set Mobile to Guessing,* Mobile, 1928.

The Mobile Commercial Register and Patriot, Tuesday, May 13, 1834, p. 2, col. 1

The Mobile Commercial Register and Patriot, *Murder!!!! $500 Reward,* May 12, p. 2, col. 5,

The Mobile Commercial Register and Patriot, May 14, 1835

The Mobile Sunday Register, 26 July 1931, p. 2

Weekly Register, Mobile, August 8, 1879

Statements

Boyington, Charles R. S., Printed at the Office of *The Mercantile Advertiser, Trial of Charles R. S. Boyington,* written by himself, 1835

Various Miscellaneous Sources

Collection of Cemetery Inscriptions and Newspaper Notices

Crime and Punishment in Antebellum Mobile

Landmark Hall Clipping Collection, 9 August 1879

Ordinance, 1826 Section 07, City of Mobile Ordinance

Websites/Internet

Encyclopediaofalabama.org,, Padgett, Charles

Encyclopediaofnorthcarolina.org, Blaufaub, Rafe, p.40

Neworleansbar.org

Theserpentsofbienville.com, blog-index/2015/10/17boyington-oak

www.genealogy.com/forum/surnames/topics/boyington/98

www.poets.org

OBSERVATIONS BY JOHN M. TYSON, JR.

In 1884, my great-grandfather, Judge John R. Tyson, heard a case in Hayneville, Alabama. In it, the defense lawyer, J.C. Richardson, referred to the Boyington trial saying that circumstantial evidence could render a questionable verdict. His concerns rose from the fact that 60 years after Boyington's guilty verdict and hanging, a woman on her deathbed confessed to the murder of Nathaniel Frost. These events changed the way circumstantial evidence is viewed. There is no question but that the result in Boyington's case would be considerably different if the trial were tried today. Not only would the verdict have been reversed on any one of the issues raised during the court proceedings concerning juror qualifications, but he would also probably have been acquitted based upon the weakness of the evidence against him. Given Boyington's age at the time of the crime and lack of criminal history, it is also likely that today he would be granted "Youthful Offender" status and not at risk of death. If a death sentence were imposed today, there would certainly be a constitutional challenge to a 19-year-old's execution as "cruel and unusual punishment." Under today's law, he would not be executed until all appeals were exhausted, which could take as much as twenty-five years or longer. I was enthralled with learning about my great-grandfather's involvement. I never knew about that before. The book has a broad appeal. It is an intriguing read for people interested in the justice system and capital punishment.

John M. Tyson, Jr., former Mobile County District Attorney and State School Board Vice President.

ABOUT THE AUTHOR

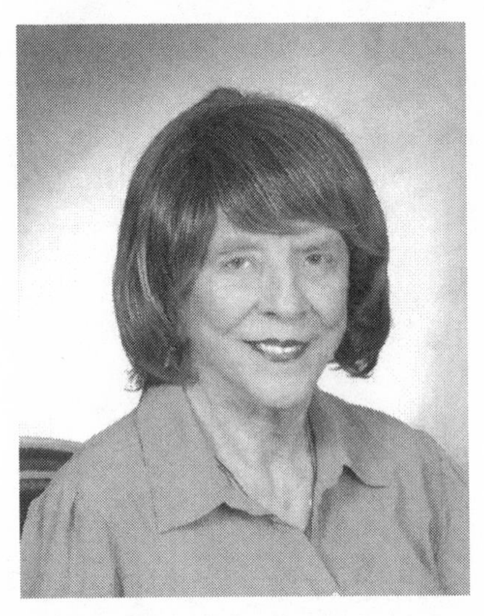

Mary S. Palmer, of Mobile, AL, has a BA (Cum Laude) in English from the University of South Alabama. Her Master's Degree is also in English with a Concentration in Creative Writing. She teaches English at Faulkner University and is a member of the adjunct faculty at Huntingdon College. She has published fifteen books, numerous poems and has had three plays produced. *Tourism Writing – A New Literary Genre Unveiling the History, Mystery, and Economy of Places and Events*, written with a Grant from Faulkner University, was released in 2018. Her short story *The Concrete Block Wall* won the Hackney Award in 2016. *Commas for Soul Searchers*, her short story collection, was released in 2021. She is currently completing a murder-mystery series.

For presentations and book signings contact
www.maryspalmer.com or email mlsp0121@gmail.com

Made in the USA
Columbia, SC
01 March 2022